A New Owner's
Guide to
CHIHUAHUAS

JG-152

The author acknowledges the contribution of Judy Iby for the following chapters: Sport of Purebred Dogs, Behavior and Canine Communication, Health Care, Identification, Finding the Lost Dog, and Traveling With your Dog.

Photo Credits:
Braun, Paulette: 14, 16, 75, 123, 124, 125
Francais, Isabelle: 7, 8, 10, 11, 13, 15, 17, 21, 22, 24, 25, 26, 27, 29, 30, 32, 37, 39, 42, 45, 47, 55, 56, 58, 59, 62, 63, 64, 66, 69, 71, 77, 78, 81, 82, 84, 85, 87, 88, 89, 90, 91, 93, 95, 102, 108, 109, 112, 115, 117, 128, 129, 131, 133, 135, 137, 138, 145, 146

T.F.H. Publications, Inc.
One TFH Plaza
Third and Union Avenues
Neptune City, NJ 07753

This book has been published with the intent to provide accurate and authoritative information in regard to the subject matter within. While every precaution has been taken in preparation of this book, the author and publisher expressly disclaim responsibility for any errors, omissions, or adverse effects arising from the use or application of the information contained herein. The techniques and suggestions are used at the reader's discretion and are not to be considered a substitute for veterinary care. If you suspect a medical problem, consult your veterinarian.

ISBN 0-7938-2801-5

www.tfhpublications.com

A New Owner's
Guide to
CHIHUAHUAS

Marion G. Mondshine

Contents

2005 Edition

Chihuahuas make great watchdogs due to their alert and inquisitive natures.

The longhaired Chihuahua has a regal and majestic bearing.

Grooming time is an opportunity to bond with your Chihuahua.

The well-socialized Chihuahua will get along with other dogs.

Many Chihuahuas enjoy and excel in agility competition.

HISTORY of the Chihuahua

ANCIENT HISTORY

As fascinating as they might be, there are far too many strange and exotic tales surrounding the origin of the Chihuahua to present in this book. Furthermore, few if any of these stories have any documented basis, and they are really nothing more than myths. What is fact, however, is that as surprising as it may seem, all dogs—from the smallest to the tallest—descend from one or more branches of the same ancestor. That ancestor is none other than *Canis lupus*—the wolf.

It may seem incongruous that the ancestors of the 5-pound Chihuahua sitting on your sofa actually roamed the forests, bringing down huge prehistoric beasts for food. However, scientific research proves this to be so.

It is difficult to pinpoint exactly when the wolf began to leave the forest and join man in his encampments, but most historians agree that it was sometime during the Mesolithic period more than 10,000 years ago. As early humans and wolves began to develop a mutually advantageous relationship, it became increasingly easy for man to observe that these wolves had individual physical and mental capabilities that could be useful to him. With the passing of time, early humans also began to realize that they could manipulate breedings of these wolves/dogs so that the resulting offspring would be extremely proficient in particular areas.

As human populations developed a more sophisticated lifestyle, their needs became far more diversified. Customizing the evolving wolves to suit these growing human needs was inevitable. The wolves became hunters, guardians, and stock drovers, and the ways in which these companions became useful were as diversified as the human population itself.

As human settlements and encampments developed into towns and villages, life became easier and mankind found time to devote to pursuits other than survival. By this time, man's personal wolves had evolved through selective breeding into a species so different they could be classified as *Canis familiaris*—domestic dog. Eventually

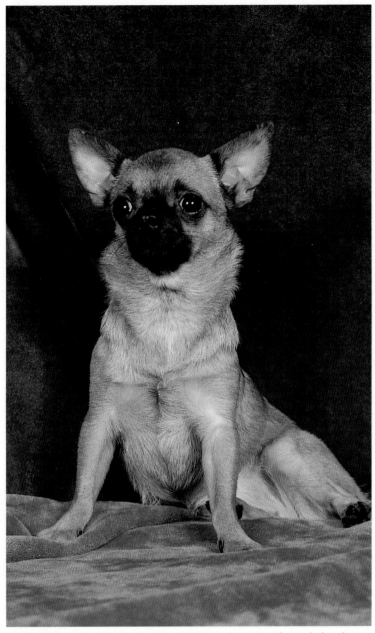

Companion and toy breeds, like the Chihuahua, have existed even before dynastic times in Egypt.

The development of the Chihuahua's ancestors is considered one of the Aztecs' many artistic triumphs.

some of the dogs were kept with no duties other than companionship or perhaps to provide an occasional warning bark when they suspected an intruder was invading their household.

There is documentation of controlled breeding practices by the Romans as early as the first century AD. The Romans had categorized the many types of dogs into six general classifications. These categories are strikingly similar to the "variety groups" used as a classification method by the American Kennel Club (AKC) today. Roman writers talked of "house guardian dogs, shepherd dogs, sporting dogs, war dogs, scent dogs, and sight dogs" 2,000 years ago. Many of today's breeds can trace their ancestry directly back to breeds that were included in those early groups.

Through the ages, most wolves and wild dogs were large and dark in color. Man's sophistication brought a desire for something "different," and humans developed an admiration for smaller, lighter-colored dogs. Dogs who were once primarily under the jurisdiction of the male population were also moving into homes and becoming the property of women as well. Also, space constraints in developing cities made it increasingly difficult to house large dogs, and those who required the companionship of a dog found need for animals who demanded less space. Thus, small dogs became very popular, and in many households they became members of the family.

Companion and toy breeds are known to have existed even before dynastic times in Egypt. According to Richard and Alice Fiennes, authors of *The Natural History of Dogs*, interest in smaller dogs developed almost simultaneously throughout the increasingly sophisticated world. The Fiennes draw a parallel in this development and point out the amazing similarities between the ancient "ha pa" dogs of China and those kept by the Aztec and Inca Indians. The regions where the Indians resided are what are known today as the countries of the upper regions of South America and Mexico.

These dogs were used in both China and among the Indian tribes of the Americas for ceremonial purposes such as living sacrifice, as well as for food consumption. Those were very small dogs, though in no way near the diminutive size of today's Chihuahua. It appears, however, that among the Aztecs' many artistic triumphs, they were particularly successful in their attempts to miniaturize their dogs.

By the early 1300s, the previously nomadic Aztecs eventually settled and developed the area of what is now known as Mexico

City. It is here that the Spanish conquistadors founded the Aztec civilization as they began their efforts to conquer the Americas.

The late Chihuahua authority and historian Thelma Gray believes that a small black and tan dog of terrier type accompanied the Spanish invaders from their native homeland. Gray's research led her to believe that it was the cross of the native dog of the Aztecs and the Spanish terrier-type dog who serves as the basis for the Chihuahua of today.

THE CHIHUAHUA GETS HIS NAME

In the mid-1800s, travelers from the US touring Mexico became enchanted with the tiny little dogs who were found along the Arizona and Texas borders. A number of them were purchased in and around the Mexican state of Chihuahua and brought back to the US. They were given the name "Chihuahua" simply because they came from that region of Mexico.

CHIHUAHUAS IN THE UNITED STATES

The earliest Chihuahuas in the US were of both coats—smooth and long. Their size and overall look varied considerably. The one

The earliest Chihuahuas in the United States were of both long and smooth coats.

The modern Chihuahua gets his name from that region of Mexico where he originated.

thing that they all did have in common was an unusual opening or soft spot at the top of the skull. This was known as the Chihuahua molera.

The AKC first listed Chihuahuas as having been exhibited at their shows in the American Kennel Club Studbook of 1890. The breed was slow in gaining public favor, and it was not until 1904 that the first Chihuahua was registered with the AKC. This dog, Midget, was bred and owned by H. Raynor of El Paso, Texas. There were only four Chihuahuas registered that year.

The first AKC champion in the breed was Mrs. L.A. McLean's Beppie, whose championship was recorded in 1908. In 1915 the total number of Chihuahuas registered was 30. Almost 50 more years passed before interest in the breed really took hold.

The earliest pioneers of the breed were Mrs. Ida Garrett, Mrs. Charles Dobbs, Charles Stewart, Mrs. L. McLean, Mrs. C. Atwood, Mrs. Ann Radcliffe, and Mrs. Bertha Peaster.

It was through their efforts that the Chihuahua Club of America was organized in 1923. Their work brought the breed to such a degree of national prominence that in 1964, more than 40,000 Chihuahuas were registered with the AKC. Since then the breed has continually held a prominent position among all breeds registered with the AKC.

The first independently held Chihuahua Specialty Show took place in 1946 and was judged by Forest N. Hall of Dallas, Texas. The winner was Ch. Meronette Grudier.

The first Chihuahua to win an all-breed Best in Show was the smooth coat Ch. Attas' Gretchen, bred and owned by Mrs. Mike Attas. It was not until 1975 that a long coat was to achieve this award, Martha Hooks' Ch. Snow Bunny d'Casa de Cris.

STANDARD for the Chihuahua

The American Kennel Club and Kennel Club standards for the Chihuahua are written in simple, straightforward language that can be read and understood by even the beginning fancier. However, their implications take many years to fully understand. This can only be accomplished by observing many quality Chihuahuas over the years and by reading as much about the breed as possible. Many books have been written about the breed, and it will be well worth your time and effort to digest their contents if you are interested in showing or breeding this dog.

There are some breeds that change drastically from puppyhood to adulthood. It would be extremely difficult for the untrained eye to determine the actual breed of some purebred dogs during puppyhood. This is not quite so with the Chihuahua, outside of the length of the mature dog's coat in the long coat variety.

How closely an individual dog adheres to the standard of the breed determines his show potential.

The Chihuahua's balanced overall construction permits graceful, easy movement.

Keep in mind that a breed standard describes the "perfect" Chihuahua, and although that is what we all hope we will one day have, no dog is perfect. Not even the greatest dog show winner will possess every quality asked for in its perfect form. It is how closely an individual dog adheres to the standard of the breed that determines his show potential.

Size is very important, as the Chihuahua is a toy breed—a lap dog. The show- and breeding-quality Chihuahua is always fewer than 6 pounds in weight. There is no such thing as a "teacup," "deer," or "cobby" variety. Pet breeders create these names to conform to their poor specimens.

Just because the Chihuahua is a toy breed does not mean there is no reason for him to be unsound. Both the American Kennel Club and Kennel Club's standards require well-made limbs and an easy way of moving. The breed's balanced construction permits graceful, easy movement.

General Appearance
A graceful, alert, swift-moving little dog with saucy expression, compact, and with terrier-like qualities of temperament.

Size, Proportion, Substance
Weight—A well balanced little dog not to exceed 6 pounds.

Proportion—The body is off-square; hence, slightly longer when measured from point of shoulder to point of buttocks, than height at the withers. Somewhat shorter bodies are preferred in males.

Disqualification—Any dog over 6 pounds in weight.

Head
A well rounded "apple dome" skull, with or without molera.

Expression—Saucy.

Eyes—Full, but not protruding, balanced, set well apart—luminous dark or luminous ruby. (Light eyes in blond or white-colored dogs permissible.)

Ears—Large, erect type ears, held more upright when alert, but

The Chihuahua should have a well-rounded "apple dome" skull, with or without a molera.

The Chihuahua features a moderately short, slightly pointed muzzle; his cheeks and jaws are lean.

flaring to the sides at a 45-degree angle when in repose, giving breadth between the ears.

Muzzle—Moderately short, slightly pointed. Cheeks and jaws lean.

Nose—Self-colored in blond types, or black. In moles, blues, and chocolates, they are self-colored. In blond types, pink nose permissible.

Bite—Level or scissors. Overshot or undershot bite, or any distortion of the bite or jaw, should be penalized as a serious fault.

Disqualifications—Broken down or cropped ears.

Neck, Topline, Body

Neck—Slightly arched, gracefully sloping into lean shoulders.

Topline—Level.

Body—Ribs rounded and well sprung (but not too much "barrel-shaped").

Tail—Moderately long, carried sickle either up or out, or in a loop over the back, with tip just touching the back. (Never tucked between legs.)

Disqualifications—Cropped tail, bobtail.

Forequarters

Shoulders—Lean, sloping into a slightly broadening support above straight forelegs that set well under, giving a free play at the elbows. Shoulders should be well up, giving balance and soundness, sloping into a level back. (Never down or low.) This gives a chestiness and strength of forequarters, yet not of the "Bulldog" chest.

Feet—A small, dainty foot with toes well split up but not spread, pads cushioned. (Neither the hare nor the cat foot.)

Pasterns—Fine.

Hindquarters

Muscular, with hocks well apart, neither out nor in, well let down, firm and sturdy. The feet are as in front.

The Chihuahua's shoulders should lend a sense of balance and soundness, sloping into a level back.

According to the AKC breed standard, the Chihuahua's coat can be any color, either solid, marked, or splashed.

Coat

In the Smooth Coats, the coat should be of soft texture, close and glossy. (Heavier coats with undercoats permissible.) Coat placed well over body with ruff on neck preferred, and more scanty on head and ears. Hair on tail preferred furry. In Long Coats, the coat should be of a soft texture, either flat or slightly curly, with undercoat preferred.

Ears—Fringed. (Heavily fringed ears may be tipped slightly if due to the fringes and not to weak ear leather, never down.)

Tail—Full and long (as a plume). Feathering on feet and legs, pants on hind legs and large ruff on the neck desired and preferred.

Disqualification—In Long Coats, too thin coat that resembles bareness.

Color

Any color—Solid, marked or splashed.

Gait

The Chihuahua should move swiftly with a firm, sturdy action, with good reach in front equal to the drive from the rear. From the rear, the hocks remain parallel to each other, and the foot fall of the rear legs follows directly behind that of the forelegs. The legs, both front and rear, will tend to converge slightly toward a central line of gravity as speed increases. The side view shows good, strong drive in the rear and plenty of reach in the front, with head carried high. The topline should remain firm and the backline level as the dog moves.

Temperament

Alert, with terrier-like qualities.

Disqualifications

Any dog over 6 pounds in weight. Broken down or cropped ears.

Cropped tail, bobtail. In Long Coats, too thin coat that resembles bareness.

—Approved September 11, 1990
—Effective October 30, 1990

THE KENNEL CLUB BREED STANDARD

General Appearance
Small, dainty, compact.

Characteristics
Alert little dog; swift-moving with brisk, forceful action and saucy expression.

Temperament
Gay, spirited and intelligent, neither snappy nor withdrawn.

Head and Skull
Well rounded "apple dome" skull, cheeks and jaws lean, muzzle moderately short, slightly pointed. Definite stop.

Eyes
Large, round, but not protruding; set well apart; centre of eye is on a plane with lowest point of ear and base of stop; dark or ruby. Light eyes in light colours permissible.

Ears
Large, flaring, set on at an angle of approximately 45 degrees; giving breadth between ears. Tipped or broken down highly undesirable.

Mouth
Jaws strong, with a perfect, regular and complete scissor bite, i.e. upper teeth closely overlapping lower teeth and set square to the jaws.

Neck
Slightly arched, medium length.

Forequarters
Shoulders well laid; lean, sloping into slightly broadening support above straight forelegs, set well under chest giving freedom of movement without looseness.

Body
Level back. Body, from point of shoulder to rear point of croup,

The Chihuahua's feet should be small and dainty, turning neither in nor out, with moderately short nails.

slightly longer than height at withers. Well sprung ribs, deep brisket.

Hindquarters
Muscular; hocks well let down, with good turn of stifle, well apart, turning neither in nor out.

Feet
Small and dainty, turning neither in nor out; toes well divided but not spread, pads cushioned, fine, strong, flexible pasterns. Neither hare- nor cat-like, nails moderately short.

Tail
Medium length, set high, carried up and over back (sickle tail). When moving never tucked under or curled below the topline. Furry, flattish in appearance, broadening slightly in centre and tapering to point.

The American Kennel Club breed standard classifies the Chihuahua's temperament as alert, with terrier-like qualities.

Gait/Movement

Brisk, forceful action, neither high-stepping nor hackney; good reach without slackness in forequarters, good drive in hindquarters. Viewed from front and behind legs should move neither too close nor too wide, with no turning in or out of feet or pasterns. Topline should remain firm and level when moving.

Coat

Long Coat: soft texture (never coarse or harsh to touch), either flat or slightly wavy. Never tight and curly. Feathering on ears, feet and legs, pants on hindquarters, large ruff on neck desirable. Tail long and full as a plume.

Smooth Coat: smooth, of soft texture, close and glossy, with undercoat and ruff permissible.

Colour

Any colour or mixture of colours.

Size

Weight: up to 2.7 kgs (6 lbs), with 1-1.8 kgs (2-4 lbs) preferred. If two dogs are equally good in type, the more diminutive preferred.

Faults

Any departure from the foregoing points should be considered a fault and the seriousness with which the fault should be regarded should be in exact proportion to its degree and its effect upon the health and welfare of the dog.

Note

Male animals should have two apparently normal testicles fully descended into the scrotum.

—March 1994

CHARACTERISTICS of the Chihuahua

The Chihuahua, the smallest of the toy breeds, has a personality and character all his own. Here is a canine in miniature who radiates personality and craves human contact. The Chihuahua asks little and gives much in return. He is the smallest, most economical, and most compact bundle of love in dogdom. He has the aggressiveness, alertness, and devotion found in no other breed. He is not a "yappy" dog, but a very inquiring and interesting little creature who will bark when his keen sense of hearing warns of the approach of a stranger. He is quiet as he scampers around the house, either playing or searching for a sunny spot in which to rest. Chihuahuas love the warmth of the sun and will spend hours basking in its rays.

The smallest of the toy breeds, the Chihuahua has a very unique temperament and personality.

24

Most Chihuahuas like to be covered when sleeping at night, so be sure to provide adequate bedding.

Though small in stature, the Chihuahua's alert nature makes him an excellent watchdog.

Never quarrelsome, Chihuahuas can live with Saint Bernards, Boxers, Newfoundlands, Great Danes, or any of the larger breeds and get along very well with them. Some people are under the impression that two male Chihuahuas cannot live together in harmony. In this particular breed, some of the most inseparable pals are males, because for a Chihuahua, no matter how pampered, spoiled, and petted, there is no such thing as not accepting a newcomer to the household. He may show a resentful attitude at first, but in a short time the first resident will welcome the newcomer and will soon be looking after him as if he were his best friend.

Most Chihuahuas like to be covered at night while they sleep. Provide them with a blanket in their bed, and they will completely cover themselves until they are hidden.

Some Chihuahuas shiver, and often an inexperienced person assumes that they are cold, even if it is a hot summer day. Shivering is often a sign of fear or is displayed by these dogs when they are wary or unhappy.

A Chihuahua who is mild-mannered in temperament may be most suited to you and your family's needs.

This toy dog has, on average, the longest life span of any group. There was once a report of a Champion attaining the ripe old age of 19. Another Chihuahua, owned by a woman in Chicago, died at the age of 18. This should provide some proof that they are a rugged breed.

TEMPERAMENT

Temperament varies in the different lines; therefore, it is important to find a line that suits your needs. Hyperactive dogs can be fun, but they require a great deal of attention and can be rather noisy. Mild-mannered dogs are quieter and more suitable for the owner who enjoys a dog who will sit quietly on his or her lap. To judge the temperament of the puppy you are considering, it is important to see and spend time with his parents and other relatives.

Although the Chihuahua would most certainly not be considered a vindictive breed, I am never surprised to hear that a Chihuahua who has been completely housetrained will suddenly forget all his manners in protest of suddenly being left alone too often or too long. Some Chihuahuas will let you know that they are not getting the attention they need by destroying household items, particularly those things that belong to the individual whom the dog is particularly devoted to—the one he is missing.

None of this should be construed to mean that only people who are home all day to cater to every whim of their dog can be Chihuahua owners. I know many working people who are away most of the day whose Chihuahuas are well mannered and trustworthy when left home alone. The key here seems to be the quality rather than quantity of time spent with their pet.

Morning or evening walks, grooming sessions, game time, and simply having your Chihuahua share your life when you are home are vital elements of the breed's personality development and attitude. A Chihuahua likes to be talked to and praised. The adage "No man is an island" applies to dogs as well, particularly in the case of the Chihuahua.

WATCHDOG

The Chihuahua is quite content to remain at home with his family, and he is not a breed prone to wander off even if he were allowed to do so. The Chihuahua is an excellent watchdog in the sense that he will sound the alarm if he sees or hears anything

Chihuahuas crave human companionship and should be talked to, praised, and petted often.

Chihuahuas are highly trainable dogs as long as they are treated with kindness and respect.

unusual. Expect your Chihuahua to let you know when the doorbell has rung or if someone is knocking at the door. This dog is keen, alert, and quick to respond. He will keep you apprised of everything and anything that he considers the least bit unusual.

TRAINABILITY

The Chihuahua makes a great effort to please his owner and is highly trainable as long as the trainer is not heavy-handed. Training problems encountered are far more apt to be due to the owner rather than a Chihuahua not understanding what is to be learned. Although many Chihuahua owners are inclined to think of their companions as "little people," they must understand that the Chihuahua is first and foremost a dog. Dogs, like the wolves from whom they descend, are pack animals and need a "pack leader." As pets, they are totally dependent upon humans to provide that leadership. When leadership is not provided, a dog can easily become confused and neurotic.

SETTING BOUNDARIES

Setting boundaries is important to the well-being of your Chihuahua and your relationship with him. The sooner your dog understands that there are rules that must be obeyed, the easier it will be for him to become an enjoyable companion. The sooner you learn to establish and enforce those rules, the quicker this will come about. As I mentioned earlier, the Chihuahua is not vindictive or particularly stubborn, but he does need guidance in order to achieve his potential.

SELECTING a Chihuahua

I f you are willing to make the necessary commitment that a Chihuahua requires, there are few breeds that are more versatile, amiable, and adaptable. Although the Chihuahua may well be the pampered pet of some owners who treat him like a china doll, the breed is hardier than one might think.

If purchased from a responsible breeder, a Chihuahua is seldom prone to chronic illnesses. Though of diminutive size, this does not mean a Chihuahua must be treated as if made of eggshells. For its size, the breed has amazing energy and great strength. With proper instruction, children old enough to understand how to handle a small dog can learn to enjoy the exuberant personality of the Chihuahua, and the dog in turn will love the gentle child.

The breed is extremely playful and inquisitive, and it is one that never ceases to have something to do. However, a Chihuahua is just as content to sit by your side when you read or listen to music. Introduced early enough and properly supervised, the Chihuahua

Chihuahuas are extremely playful and inquisitive, and they tend to have high energy levels.

can coexist with your cat, rabbit, or even a larger dog as well as he can with humans. And it can be said without hesitation that two Chihuahuas are just as easy to raise as one.

The important thing to remember, though, is that the breed is an aggressive one and inclined to be somewhat bossy. This can come as a challenge to other breeds not inclined to overlook the Chihuahua's feisty attitude.

MAKING THE DECISION

Before you try to decide whether or not the Chihuahua is the correct breed for you, a larger, more important question must be asked: "Should I own any dog at all?" Dog ownership is a serious and time-consuming responsibility that should not be entered into lightly. Failure to understand this can make what should be a rewarding relationship into one of sheer drudgery. It is also one of the primary reasons for the euthanization of thousands of unwanted dogs by humane societies and animal shelters throughout the US.

Do not think for a moment that the tiny size of a Chihuahua will relieve you of the responsibilities that dog ownership involves. In some instances the breed's size requires even more consideration.

If the prospective dog owner lives alone and conditions are conducive to dog ownership, all he or she needs to do is to be sure that there is a strong desire to make the necessary commitment that dog ownership entails. In the case of family households, the situation is much more complicated. It is essential that the person who will actually be responsible for the dog's care really wants a dog.

Nearly all children love puppies and dogs and will promise anything to get one. However, childhood enthusiasm can wane very quickly, and it will be up to the adults in the family to ensure that the dog receives proper care. Children should be taught responsibility, but to expect a living, breathing, and needy animal to teach a child this lesson is incredibly indifferent to the needs of the animal.

Should an individual or family find they are capable of providing the proper home for a dog or young puppy, suitability of the breed must also be considered. Here it might be worthwhile to look at the difference between owning a purebred dog and owning one of mixed ancestry.

Mixed Breed or Purebred?

A mixed breed can give you as much love and devotion as a purebred dog. However, the manner in which the dog does this and how his personality, energy level, and the amount of care he requires suits an individual's lifestyle are major considerations. In a purebred dog, most of these considerations are predictable to a marked degree even if the dog is purchased as a very young puppy. A puppy of uncertain parentage will not give you this assurance.

All puppies are cute and fairly manageable, but someone who lives in a two-room apartment will find life difficult with a dog who will grow to the size of a Great Dane. Nor will owner or dog be suitable for each other if the dog is a toy breed and the owner's life is spent outdoors in the frozen north.

An owner who expects his or her dog to sit quietly while he or she watches television or reads is not going to be particularly happy with a high-strung, off-the-wall dog whose rest requirements are only 30 seconds out of every 10 hours!

Toy breed puppies are very fragile and need to be handled with care, especially by children.

Toy breed puppies are very fragile and can be easily injured by unthinking children. Rambunctious puppies of the very large breeds can just as easily injure a toddler. Knowing what kind of dog best suits your lifestyle is not just a consideration—it is paramount to the foundation of your lifelong relationship with the dog. If the dog you are considering does not fit your lifestyle, the relationship simply will not last.

Male or Female?

Although in many breeds of dog the sex is a very important consideration, this is not particularly the case with the Chihuahua. Males make just as loving, devoted, and trainable companions as females. In fact, there are some who believe that a male can be even more devoted to his family than a female.

There is one important point to consider in choosing between a male and female. While both must be trained not to relieve themselves in the home, males have a natural instinct to lift their leg and "mark" their home territory. While it may seem confusing to many dog owners, a male marking his home turf has absolutely nothing to do with whether or not he is housetrained. The two responses come from entirely different needs and must be dealt with in that manner. Some dogs are more difficult to train not to mark within the confines of the household than others. Males who are used for breeding are more prone to this response and are even harder to train not to do so.

On the other hand, females have their semiannual "heat" cycles once they have reached sexual maturity. In the case of the female Chihuahua, this can occur for the first time at about nine or ten months of age. These cycles are accompanied by a vaginal discharge that creates the need to confine the female for about three weeks so she does not soil her surroundings. It must be understood that the female has no control over this discharge and it has nothing to do with training. Needless to say, the female in heat should not be left outdoors by herself for even a brief moment or two. The need for confinement and keeping a careful watch over the female in heat is especially important to prevent her from becoming pregnant by some neighborhood Lothario. Equally dangerous to her well-being is the male who is much larger than the female Chihuahua. The dog may be too large to actually breed her, but he could seriously injure or even kill her in his attempts to do so.

Puppy or Adult?

For the person anticipating a show career for his or her Chihuahua, or for someone hoping to become a breeder, the purchase of a young adult provides greater certainty with respect to quality. Even those who simply want a companion should consider the adult dog.

From a breeder's point of view, Chihuahuas act like puppies their entire lives and readily adapt to new places and people quite easily. In some instances, breeders will have males or females they no longer wish to use for breeding and would prefer to have them live out their lives in a private home with lots of care and attention. In the private home environment, the dog will become the "one and only" instead of "one of many."

Acquiring an adult dog eliminates the many problems involved in raising a puppy, and Chihuahuas, unlike some other breeds, do transfer well. They love to be with humans, and although many of us hate to admit it, most Chihuahuas would be just as content living with one person as they are with another—just as long as they are loved and well cared for.

Elderly people often prefer the adult dog, particularly one who is housetrained, because adult dogs are easier to manage and require less supervision and damage control. Adult Chihuahuas are seldom chewers and are usually more than ready to adapt to household rules.

There are things to consider, though. Adult dogs have usually developed behaviors that may or may not fit into your routine. If a Chihuahua has never been exposed to children, the dog may be totally perplexed and often frightened by this new experience. Children are also inclined to be more active and vocal than the average adult, and this could intimidate the dog as well.

I strongly advise taking an adult dog on a trial basis to see if he will adapt to the new owner's lifestyle and environment. Most often it works, but on rare occasions a prospective owner may decide that training his or her dog from puppyhood is worth the time and effort required.

FINDING A BREEDER

The Chihuahua you purchase will live with you for many years to come. It is not the least bit unusual for the well-bred Chihuahua to live as long as 15 to 18 years of age. Obviously, it is important that your Chihuahua comes from sound, healthy stock; it is also

Responsible breeders base their breeding programs on the healthiest, most representative stock available.

important that he has the advantage of beginning life in a healthy environment.

The only way you can be sure of this is to go directly to someone who has earned a reputation over the years for consistently producing Chihuahuas who are mentally and physically sound. A breeder is able to earn this reputation only through a well-planned breeding program that has been governed by rigid selectivity. Selective breeding programs are aimed at maintaining the many fine qualities of the breed and eliminating any genetic weaknesses.

This process is both time consuming and costly for a breeder, but it ensures the buyer of getting a dog who will be a joy to own. Responsible Chihuahua breeders protect their investment by basing their breeding programs on the healthiest, most representative stock available and by providing each succeeding generation with the very best care and nutrition.

The governing kennel clubs in different countries maintain lists of local breed clubs and breeders that can lead a prospective Chihuahua buyer to responsible breeders of quality stock. If you are not sure where to contact an established Chihuahua breeder in your area, I strongly recommend contacting your local all-breed kennel club or a Chihuahua club in your area for recommendations.

Questions for Breeder and Buyer

It is likely that you will be able to find an established Chihuahua breeder in your own area. If so, you will be able to visit the breeder, inspect the premises, and in many cases, see a puppy's parents and other relatives. These breeders are always willing and able to discuss any problems that might exist in the breed and how they should be dealt with.

If there are no breeders in your immediate area, you can arrange to have a puppy shipped to you. There are breeders throughout the country who have shipped puppies to satisfied owners out of state and even to other countries.

Never hesitate to ask the breeder any questions or concerns you might have about owning a Chihuahua. You should expect the breeder to ask you a good number of questions as well. Good breeders are just as interested in placing their puppies in a loving and safe environment as you are in obtaining a happy, healthy puppy.

A responsible breeder will want to know if there are young children in the family and what their ages are. He or she will also want to know if you or your children have ever owned a dog before. The breeder will want to know if you live in an apartment or in a home. If you live in a home, they will want to know if you have a fenced-in yard and if there will be someone home during the day to attend to a young puppy's needs.

Not all good breeders maintain large kennels. In fact, you are more apt to obtain Chihuahuas from small hobby breeders who only keep a few dogs and have litters only occasionally. The names of these people are just as likely to appear on the recommended lists from kennel clubs as the larger kennels that maintain many dogs. Hobby breeders are equally dedicated to breeding quality Chihuahuas and have the distinct advantage of being able to raise their puppies in the home environment with all of its accompanying personal attention and socialization.

Again, it is important that both the buyer and seller ask questions. You should be highly suspicious of a person who is willing to sell you a Chihuahua puppy with no questions asked.

CHOOSING A PUPPY

There are two coat varieties in Chihuahuas—long coats and smooth coats. The long coats have coats that are soft in texture,

Never hesitate to ask the breeder any questions you may have; a good breeder will be more than willing to address your concerns.

either flat or slightly curly, with undercoat preferred. They have thick fringes on the tail, legs, and ears. Males have a larger ruff around the neck than do the females. A little more time and effort must be spent on the long coats in order to keep them neat, tidy, and tangle-free. Other than the length of the coat, the standard requirements for the two varieties are exactly the same.

Most Chihuahua breeders are apt to keep their puppies until they are 10 to 12 weeks of age and have been given all of their puppy inoculations. By the time the puppy is this old, he is entirely weaned—no longer nursing on his mother. While puppies are nursing, they have at least partial immunity from infectious diseases. Once they reach a certain age, however, they become highly susceptible to these diseases. A number of diseases can be transmitted on the hands and clothing of humans. Therefore, it is extremely important that your puppy is up to date on all the shots he must have for his age.

Most Chihuahua puppies are bouncy, playful extroverts. This is particularly so when the breeder has taken the time to begin the socialization process while the puppies are still in the nest. Never select a puppy who appears shy or listless just because you feel sorry for him. Doing so will undoubtedly lead to heartache and expensive veterinary costs. Do not attempt to make up for what the breeder did not accomplish in terms of providing proper care and nutrition. It seldom works.

This is not to say that quieter puppies have bad temperaments. Give the quieter puppy an opportunity to warm up to you. However, never select a puppy who appears terrified at the sight of a stranger.

Always ask the breeder if you may pick up the puppy you are attracted to and take him into a different room in the kennel or house. The smells will remain the same for the puppy, so he should still feel secure, but it will give you an opportunity to see how the puppy acts away from his littermates. It will also give you time to inspect the puppy more closely.

Physical Characteristics

Check for the "molera," which is a small opening on top of the skull. It approximates the fontanel that human babies are born with. In humans, this opening closes within the first year. Some Chihuahuas, on the other hand, retain this characteristic for their

While almost all puppies are born with a molera, it usually closes by the time they reach adulthood.

entire lives. In any case, the opening should be small. Years ago it was a requirement in the AKC standard that the Chihuahua have this soft spot on the head. Today's standard states, "Head—a well rounded 'apple dome' skull, with or without molera." Almost all puppies have a molera, but it usually closes by adulthood. Some veterinarians who are unfamiliar with the breed may misdiagnose a puppy with a molera as being hydrocephalic (which means "water on the brain"). This is not true—a completely healthy Chihuahua pup can have a molera. A hydrocephalic puppy or adult will feature an unusually large domed head.

Even though Chihuahua puppies are very small, they should feel sturdy to the touch. They should not feel bony, and their abdomens should not be bloated and extended. A puppy who has just eaten may have a belly that is full, but the puppy should never appear obese.

A healthy puppy's ears will be pink and clean. Dark discharge or a bad odor could indicate ear mites—a sure sign of poor maintenance and lack of cleanliness. A Chihuahua puppy's breath should always smell sweet. His teeth must be clean and bright, and there should

Healthy Chihuahua puppies should feel strong and sturdy to the touch, not bony or obese.

never be a malformation of the jaw, lips, or nostrils. A Chihuahua's eyes are bright and clear and large and open, never slanted in appearance. Runny eyes or eyes that appear red and irritated could be caused by a myriad of problems, none of which indicate a healthy puppy.

Coughing and diarrhea are danger signs, as is any discharge from the nose or eruptions on the skin. The skin should be clean and the coat soft, clean, and lustrous. Also, check the puppy's teeth. They should meet in what is called a scissor bite, in which the inside surfaces of the upper incisors touch the outside surfaces of the lower incisors. Overshot or undershot bites usually grow worse with age.

Sound conformation can be determined even at eight or ten weeks of age. The puppy's legs should be straight, without bumps or malformations. The toes should point straight ahead.

The puppy's attitude will tell you a great deal about his state of health. Puppies who are feeling out of sorts react very quickly and will usually find a warm littermate to snuggle up to. They will prefer to stay that way even when the rest of the gang wants to play or go exploring.

CHOOSING A SHOW PROSPECT PUPPY

What do we want a show puppy to look like? Why, just like the perfect Chihuahua, of course! Although this is what we all want, perfection is impossible to achieve. Puppies go through so many developmental stages that my best advice would be to have as much age as possible on the puppy before making any decisions. Certainly he should be six months or older. By that time it will be possible to evaluate conformation.

There is an old saying in the breed that at birth every puppy in a litter is a Best in Show winner; at six weeks, they are all Group winners; at six months, they are all Champions; and at a year, all of them are simply good pets.

If you or your family is considering a show career for your puppy, I strongly advise putting yourself in the hands of an established breeder who has earned a reputation for breeding winning show dogs. Established breeders are most capable of anticipating what one might expect a young puppy of their line to develop into when he reaches maturity.

Although the potential buyer should read the AKC or KC standard of perfection for the Chihuahua, it is hard for the novice to really understand the nuances of what is being asked for. The experienced breeder is best equipped to do so and will be happy to assist you in your quest. However, no one can make accurate predictions or guarantees on a very young puppy.

Any predictions a breeder is apt to make are based upon the breeder's experience with past litters that produced winning show dogs. It should be obvious that the more successful a breeder has been in producing winning Chihuahuas through the years, the broader his basis of comparison will be.

There are many "beauty point" shortcomings a Chihuahua puppy might have that would in no way interfere with him being a wonderful companion, but these faults would be serious drawbacks in the show ring. Many of these flaws are such that a beginner in the breed would hardly notice. Things such as lack of pigment, one or no testicles for a male, an ear that does not stand erect in an older puppy, or a dog who will mature to more than 6 pounds in weight would not keep your Chihuahua from being a happy, healthy, and loving companion. These same things, however, would keep him from ever being a winner. This is why employing the assistance of a good breeder is so important. Still, the prospective buyer should be at least generally aware of what the Chihuahua show puppy should look like.

All of the foregoing regarding soundness and health of the pet puppy applies to the show puppy as well. The show prospect must not only be sound and healthy, but he must adhere to the standard of the breed very closely.

At six months of age, a Chihuahua puppy will indicate whether or not he will wind up within the 6-pound weight limit. The beginning of a good coat in a long coat puppy will usually be discernible at this point. Mental and physical soundness can be observed as well. The Chihuahua puppy's back should be strong and straight. The tail is a curved sickle carried up and either curving or looped over the back. The ears appear quite large for the puppy's head.

Like the pet, the show-prospect puppy must have a happy, outgoing temperament. He will be a compact little bundle of energy that will rarely appear out of balance. Still, there are some bloodlines that do experience an awkward stage, and if this seems to be the condition of a puppy you are considering, mention it to the breeder. The show puppy will move around with ease and an "I love the world" attitude.

The complete standard of the breed appears in this book, and there are also a number of other books that can assist the newcomer in learning more about the Chihuahua. The more you know about the history and origin of the breed and the breed standard itself, the better equipped you will be to see the differences that distinguish the show dog from the pet.

IMPORTANT PAPERS

The purchase of any purebred dog entitles you to some very important documents, including a health record that contains an inoculation or shot record, a copy of the dog's pedigree, the registration certificate, and a health guarantee. Many breeders will also provide you with a diet sheet, which is a record of the amount and type of food the puppy has been eating.

Health Record

You will find that most Chihuahua breeders have initiated the necessary preliminary inoculation series for their puppies by the time they are 12 weeks of age. These inoculations temporarily protect the puppies against hepatitis, leptospirosis, distemper, and canine parvovirus. "Permanent" inoculations will follow at a

Your Chihuahua's pedigree authenticates his ancestors back to at least the third generation.

prescribed time. Since different breeders and veterinarians follow different approaches to inoculations, it is extremely important that the health record you obtain for your puppy accurately lists what shots have been given and when the veterinarian you choose will be able to continue with the appropriate inoculation series as needed. In most cases, rabies inoculations are not given until a puppy is three to six months old, depending on local ordinances.

Pedigree

The pedigree is your dog's family tree. The breeder must supply you with a copy of this document, which authenticates your puppy's ancestors back to at least the third generation. All purebred dogs have pedigrees. The pedigree in itself does not mean that your puppy is of show quality; it just indicates that all of his ancestors were, in fact, registered Chihuahuas. (They may all have been of pet quality, however.) Unscrupulous puppy dealers often try to imply that a pedigree indicates that all dogs having one are of championship caliber. This is not true. Again, it simply tells you that all of the dog's ancestors are purebred.

Registration Certificate

The registration certificate is the canine world's birth certificate. A country's governing kennel club issues this certificate. When you transfer the ownership of your Chihuahua from the breeder's name to your own name, the transaction is entered on this certificate. Once mailed to the appropriate kennel club, the certificate is permanently recorded in their computerized files.

Keep all of your dog's documents in a safe place. You will need them when you visit your veterinarian or if you ever wish to breed or show your Chihuahua. Keep the name, address, and phone number of the breeder from whom you purchase your Chihuahua in a separate place. Should you ever lose any of these important documents, contact the breeder about obtaining duplicates.

Health Guarantee

Any reputable breeder should be more than willing to supply a written agreement that the purchase of your Chihuahua is contingent upon his passing a veterinarian's examination. Ideally, you will be able to arrange an appointment with your chosen veterinarian right after you have picked up your puppy from the breeder and before you take the puppy home. If this is not possible, you should not delay the procedure any longer than 24 hours from the time you take your puppy home.

Diet Sheet

Your Chihuahua is the happy, healthy puppy he is because the breeder has been carefully feeding and caring for him. Every breeder I know has his or her own particular way of doing this. Most breeders give the new owner a written record that details the amount and kind of food a puppy has been receiving. Follow these recommendations to the letter, at least for the first month or two after the puppy comes to live with you.

The diet sheet should indicate the number of times a day your Chihuahua has been accustomed to being fed and the kind of vitamin supplementation, if any, he has been receiving. Following the prescribed procedure will reduce the chance of upset stomach and loose stools.

A breeder's diet sheet usually projects the increases and changes in food that will be necessary as your puppy grows from week to week. If the sheet does not include this information, ask the breeder for suggestions regarding increases and the eventual changeover to adult food.

In the unlikely event the breeder does not supply you with a diet sheet and you are unable to get one, your veterinarian will be able to advise you in this respect. There are countless foods now being manufactured expressly to meet the nutritional needs of puppies and growing dogs. A trip down the pet aisle at your supermarket will prove just how many choices you have. Two important tips to remember: Read labels carefully for content, and you get what you pay for when you deal with established, reliable manufacturers.

BRINGING YOUR NEW PUPPY HOME

At long last, the day you have been waiting for will come, and your new puppy will make his grand entrance into your home. Before you bring your companion to his new residence, however, you must plan carefully for his arrival. Keep in mind that the puppy will need time to adjust to life with a different owner. He may seem a bit apprehensive about the strange surrounding in which he finds

Careful planning will make your new companion's transition to your home much smoother.

himself, having spent the first few weeks of life with his dam and littermates. In a couple of days, with love and patience on your part, the transition will be complete.

The puppy's first impressions are important, and these feelings may very well set the pattern of his future relationship with you. You must be consistent in the way you handle your pet so that he learns what is expected of him. He must also come to trust and respect you. When you provide your Chihuahua with proper care and attention, you will be rewarded with a loyal companion for many years. If you consider the needs of your puppy before you bring him home and plan accordingly, it will make the change from his former home to his new home easier.

Advance Preparation

In preparing for your puppy's arrival, one of the most important things to find out from the seller is how the pup was maintained. What brand of food was offered, and when and how often was the puppy fed? Has the pup been housetrained? If so, what method was employed? At first, continue the routine started by the puppy's original owner; then, you can gradually make changes that suit you and your lifestyle. If, for example, the puppy has been paper trained, plan to stock up on newspaper or specially made pads. Place these in a selected spot so that your puppy learns to use the designated area as his "bathroom." If you wish to train the puppy to eliminate outdoors, you can gradually move the area closer to the door and eventually teach the puppy to go outside. Also, keep a supply of the dog food he has been eating on hand, because a sudden switch to a new food could cause digestive upsets.

Another consideration is sleeping and resting quarters. Be sure to supply a dog bed for your pup, and introduce him to his special cozy corner so that he knows where to retire when he feels like taking a snooze. A crate is a great tool to use as your puppy's sleeping quarters, and it also aids in the housetraining process. You'll need to buy a collar and leash, safe chew toys, and a few grooming tools as well. A couple of sturdy feeding dishes—one for food and one for water—will also be needed.

Children and Puppies

If you have children at home, be sure to prepare them for the arrival of their new puppy. Children should learn not only to love their charges but to respect them and treat them with the consideration that one would give all living things. It must be emphasized to youngsters that the puppy has certain needs, just as humans have, and that all family members must take an active role in ensuring that these needs are met. Someone must feed the puppy, walk him a couple of times a day, groom his coat, clean his ears, and clip his nails. Someone must also see to it that the puppy gets sufficient exercise and attention each day.

A child who has a pet to care for learns responsibility; nonetheless, parental guidance is an essential part of this learning experience. You must teach your child how to carefully pick up and handle the pup. A dog should always be supported with both hands, not lifted by the scruff of the neck. One hand should be placed under the chest, between the front legs, and the other hand should support the dog's rear end.

Be a Good Neighbor

For the sake of your dog's safety and well-being, don't allow him to wander onto your neighbors' property. Keep him confined to your own yard at all times or on his leash when outside. There are many dangers for an unleashed dog, particularly when he is unsupervised, including cars and trucks, stray animals, and poisonous substances. Also, dogs who are left to roam in a wooded area or field could become infected with any number of parasites. All of these things can be avoided if you take precautions to keep your dog in a safe enclosure where he will be protected.

Getting Acquainted

If possible, plan to bring your new pet home in the morning so that by nightfall he will have had some time to become acquainted with you and his new environment. Let the puppy enter your home on a day when the routine is normal. For those people who work during the week, a Saturday morning is an ideal time to bring the puppy to his new home.

Let the puppy explore, under your watchful eye, of course, and let him investigate his new home without stress and fear. Resist the temptation to handle him too much during these first few days. If there are other dogs or animals around the house, make certain that all are properly introduced. If you observe fighting among the animals, you may have to separate all parties until they learn to accept one another. Neglecting your other pets while showering the new puppy with extra attention will only cause animosity and jealousy. Make an effort to pay special attention to the other animals as well.

On that first night, your puppy may be frightened or lonely. It is all right to pay extra attention to him until he becomes used to his surroundings. Some people have had success with putting a doll or a hot water bottle wrapped in a towel in the puppy's bed as a surrogate mother, while others have placed a ticking alarm clock in the bed to simulate the heartbeat of the pup's dam and littermates. Remember that this furry little fellow is used to the warmth and security of his mother and siblings, so the adjustment to sleeping alone will take time. Select a sleeping location away from drafts and his feeding station. Also keep in mind that the bed should be roomy enough for him to stretch out in.

Prior to the pup's arrival, set up his room and partition it with gates or a pen to keep him in a safe enclosure. Wherever you decide to keep him, do it ahead of time so you will have that much less to worry about when your puppy finally moves in with you.

Above all else, be patient with your puppy as he adjusts to life in his new home. If you purchase a pup who is not housetrained, you will have to spend lots of time with him—just as you would with a small child—until he develops proper toilet habits. Even a housetrained puppy may feel nervous in strange new surroundings and have an occasional accident. Praise and encouragement will elicit far better results than punishment or scolding. Remember that your puppy wants nothing more than to please you, and he is anxious to learn the behavior that is required of him.

TEMPERAMENT AND SOCIALIZATION

Temperament is both hereditary and environmental. Inherited good temperament can be ruined by poor treatment and lack of proper socialization. A Chihuahua puppy who comes from shy or extremely nervous stock or one who exhibits those characteristics himself will make a poor companion or show dog and should certainly never be used for breeding. Therefore, it is critical that you obtain a happy puppy from a breeder who is determined to produce good temperaments and has taken all the necessary steps early on to provide early socialization.

Temperaments in the same litter can range from confident and outgoing on the high end of the scale to shy and fearful at the low end. The Chihuahua's temperament should generally be confident and inquisitive.

The Chihuahua is not a particularly good breed for very young children. Through no fault of their own, toddlers are usually not able to understand that something as small as a Chihuahua must be handled with care. Care must always be taken that a puppy is not dropped or squeezed hard and that he is not left to run around where he can jump off high things or where a door might close on him.

Every visitor who enters your household should be introduced to your Chihuahua; this should help your dog become accustomed to being handled by people other than yourself. You can take your puppy everywhere with you: the post office, the market, the shopping mall—wherever. Be prepared to create a stir wherever you go, because the very reason you were attracted to the first Chihuahua you met applies to other people as well. Everyone will want to pet

When selecting a puppy, look for one with a confident, inquisitive temperament.

your little companion, and there is nothing in the world better for him.

One word of caution: It is best to carry your puppy or even adult Chihuahua where there is a great deal of foot traffic. A Chihuahua can be stepped on and severely injured in situations of that kind.

If your Chihuahua has a show career in his future, there are other things in addition to just being handled that will have to be taught. All show dogs must learn to have their mouths inspected by a judge. A judge must also be able to check the teeth. Males must be accustomed to having their testicles touched, because dog show judges must determine that all male dogs are "complete," which means there are two normal size testicles in the scrotum. These inspections must begin in puppyhood and be done on a regular and continuing basis.

A Chihuahua may be entirely compatible with other dogs, but his interaction with larger dogs must be carefully supervised. Larger dogs are not aware of their own strength and can get entirely carried away in their enthusiasm to play. A Chihuahua can be too bold and challenging for his own good at times, and he can incite his larger canine friend into romping and playing in a manner that might result in an unintentional accident.

THE ADOLESCENT CHIHUAHUA

The adolescent Chihuahua seems to grow in little spurts. What once looked like a nice, compact puppy may look short-legged and longer-bodied at three to four months of age. He will usually regain his balanced proportions at maturity.

The type and amount of food needs to be changed during this growth period. Some Chihuahuas seem like they can never get enough to eat, while others eat just enough to avoid starving. Think of Chihuahua puppies as being as individualistic as children and act accordingly.

The amount of food you give your Chihuahua should be adjusted to how much he will readily consume at each meal. Though the Chihuahua is a tiny breed, he is high in energy and burns far more calories for his size than any of the very large breeds.

If the entire meal is eaten quickly, add a small amount to the next feeding, and continue to do so as the need increases. This method will ensure that you give your puppy enough food, but you must also pay close attention to the dog's appearance and condition, as you do not want a puppy to become overweight or obese.

At eight weeks of age, a Chihuahua puppy is eating four meals a day. By the time he is six months old, the puppy can do well on two meals a day with perhaps a snack in the middle of the day. If you puppy does not eat the food he is offered, he is either not hungry or not well. Your dog will eat when he is hungry. If you suspect your dog is not well, a trip to the veterinarian is immediately in order.

This adolescent period is a particularly important one because it is the time that your Chihuahua must learn all of the household and social rules by which he will live for the rest of his life. Your patience and commitment during this time will not only produce a respected canine citizen but will forge a bond between the two of you that will grow and ripen into a wonderful relationship.

CARING for Your Chihuahua

FEEDING AND NUTRITION

The best way to make sure your Chihuahua puppy is obtaining the right amount and correct type of food for his age is to follow the diet sheet provided by the breeder from whom you obtain your puppy. Do your best not to change the puppy's diet and he will be less apt to run into digestive problems and diarrhea. Diarrhea is very serious in young Chihuahua puppies. Puppies with diarrhea can dehydrate very rapidly, causing severe problems and even death.

If it is necessary to change your Chihuahua puppy's diet for any reason, it should be done gradually, over a period of several meals and a few days. Begin by adding a teaspoon or two of the new food, gradually increasing the amount until the meal consists entirely of the new product.

By the time your Chihuahua is 10 to 12 months old, you can reduce feedings to 1 or 2 a day at most. The main meal can be given either in the morning or evening. It is really a matter of choice on your part. However, there are two important things to remember: Feed the main meal at the same time every day, and make sure what you feed is nutritionally complete.

The single meal can be supplemented by a morning or nighttime snack of hard dog biscuits made especially for toy dogs. These biscuits not only become highly anticipated treats by your Chihuahua, but they are genuinely helpful in maintaining healthy gums and teeth.

"Balanced" Diets

In order for a canine diet to qualify as "complete and balanced" in the US, it must meet standards set by the Subcommittee on Canine Nutrition of the National Research Council of the National Academy of Sciences. Most commercial foods manufactured for dogs meet these standards and prove this by listing the ingredients contained in the food on every can or package. The ingredients are listed in descending order, with the main ingredient listed first.

It is best to feed your Chihuahua his meals at the same time each day to prevent stomach upset.

Fed with any regularity at all, refined sugars can cause your Chihuahua to become obese and will definitely create tooth decay. Candy stores do not exist in nature, and canine teeth are not genetically disposed to handling sugars. Do not feed your Chihuahua candy or sweets, and avoid products that contain sugar to any high degree.

Fresh water and a properly prepared, balanced diet containing the essential nutrients in correct proportions are all that a healthy Chihuahua needs for sustenance. Dog foods come canned, dry, semi-moist, "scientifically fortified," and "all-natural." A visit to your local supermarket or pet store will reveal a vast array from which you will be able to select.

It is important to remember that all dogs, whether toy or giant, are carnivorous (meat eating) animals. While the vegetable content of the Chihuahua's diet should not be overlooked, a dog's physiology and anatomy are based upon carnivorous food acquisition. Protein and fat are absolutely essential to the well-being of your Chihuahua.

Your Chihuahua needs fresh water and a properly prepared, balanced diet to remain healthy.

Read the list of ingredients on the dog food you buy. Animal protein should appear first on the label's list of ingredients. A base of quality kibble to which meat (canned or freshly cooked) has been added can provide a nutritious meal for your Chihuahua.

This having been said, it should be realized that in the wild, carnivores eat the entire beast they capture and kill. The carnivore's kills consist almost entirely of herbivorous (plant eating) animals, and invariably the carnivore begins his meal with the contents of the herbivore's stomach. This provides the carbohydrates, minerals, and nutrients present in vegetables.

We have made our dogs entirely dependent upon us for their well-being through centuries of domestication. Therefore, we are entirely responsible for duplicating the food balance that wild dogs find in nature. The domesticated dog's diet must include protein, carbohydrates, fats, roughage, and small amounts of essential minerals and vitamins.

Finding commercially prepared diets that contain all of the necessary nutrients will not present a problem. Most Chihuahua breeders recommend vitamin supplementation for a healthy coat and increased stamina, especially for show dogs, pregnant bitches, or very young puppies.

Oversupplementation

A great deal of controversy exists today regarding the orthopedic problems that afflict many breeds. Some claim these problems are entirely hereditary conditions, but many others feel they can be exacerbated by overuse of mineral and vitamin supplements for puppies. Some breeders now look upon oversupplementation as a major contributor to many skeletal abnormalities found in purebred dogs. In giving vitamin supplementation, one should never exceed the prescribed amount. No vitamin, however, is a substitute for a nutritious, balanced diet.

Pregnant and lactating bitches do require supplementation of some kind, but here again it is not a case of "if a little is good, a lot would be a great deal better." Extreme caution is advised in this case and is best discussed with your veterinarian.

Dogs do not care if food looks like a hot dog or a piece of cheese. Truly nutritious dog foods are seldom manufactured to look like the food that appeals to humans. Dogs only care about how food smells and tastes. It is highly doubtful you will be eating your dog's food, so do not waste your money on these look-alike products.

Along these lines, most of the moist foods or canned foods that have the appearance of "delicious red beef" look that way because they contain great amounts of red dyes. To test the dye content of either canned or dry foods, place a small amount of the moistened food on an absorbent towel and allow it to remain there for several hours. Preservatives and dyes are no better for your dog than they are for you.

Special Diets

There are now a number of commercially prepared diets for dogs with special dietary needs. The overweight, underweight, or geriatric dog can also have his nutritional needs met. The calorie content should help your dog stay in top shape. Again, common sense must prevail. Too many calories will increase weight, while too few will reduce weight.

Occasionally, a young Chihuahua going through the teething period will become a poor eater. The concerned owner's first response might be to tempt the dog by hand-feeding him special treats and foods that the problem eater seems to prefer. This practice will only serve to compound the problem, though. Once

Fresh, cool water should be made available to your Chihuahua at all times.

Begin grooming procedures slowly so that your Chihuahua becomes accustomed to the process.

the dog learns to play the waiting game, he will turn up his nose at anything other than his favorite food, knowing full well that what he wants to eat will eventually arrive.

A healthy dog will not starve himself to death. He may not eat enough to keep himself in the shape we find ideal and attractive, but he will definitely eat enough to maintain himself. If your Chihuahua is not eating properly and appears to be too thin, it is probably best to consult your veterinarian.

GROOMING

Getting Started

Puppyhood is the best time to start grooming procedures, because your dog will become used to the grooming routine and soon come to expect it as part of his everyday life. This is especially true if you plan to show your puppy when he gets older. It is best to start out slowly so that he doesn't become overwhelmed or frightened, and then build on grooming time until you have the whole routine down pat.

Grooming Supplies

Grooming Table

First, you may want to invest in a good grooming table. Your dog's leash can be attached to the grooming arm on the table, which will help keep him secure. Most tables have nonskid pads on the surface to keep your dog from sliding around. A grooming table can be adjusted to your height and will make it unnecessary for you to bend over or kneel down.

Introduce your puppy to the grooming table slowly. Place him on it without doing anything to him, and give him a treat when you let him down. After you do this several times, your puppy should eagerly get up on the grooming table. You can then start lightly brushing him and running any appliances, like hair dryers. When he seems comfortable, you can start grooming him on a regular basis. This gradual introduction will ensure that your puppy grows to enjoy his grooming time with you. Once your puppy is accustomed to being touched, patted, and fussed over, you can start a grooming routine that will keep him looking clean and healthy.

Slicker Brush

This versatile brush can work on many different coat types. The wire bristles grasp and remove a dogs' undercoat, help reduce shedding, and keep the coat from becoming matted.

Flea Comb

A fine-toothed flea comb will be helpful in getting hard-to-reach spots and will remove any flea or flea dirt that may be in your dog's coat.

Towels

Old towels are always handy and can be used to wipe off muddy paws and dry off wet coats.

Grooming Glove

This tool (also called a hound glove) is wonderful for dogs with short coats because it helps loosen any dead hair and gets rid of surface dirt.

Nail Clippers

Every dog needs to have his nails trimmed. A good pair of canine nail clippers will be necessary if you decide to tackle this task yourself.

Doggy Toothbrush and Toothpaste

Keeping your puppy's teeth clean is essential for maintaining his good health. Be sure to purchase toothpaste and toothbrushes that are especially made for dogs. Never use human toothpaste when brushing your dog's teeth; he will swallow it, and that can cause stomach upset and digestive problems. In addition, the minty taste that humans enjoy will not be as appealing to your puppy as it is to you. Canine toothpaste comes in "doggy-friendly" flavors, such as beef and poultry.

Shampoo

There are many brands of canine shampoo available, and some have special purposes, such as flea shampoos, medicated shampoos, and whiteners. If you are unsure about what brand to buy, ask your veterinarian for a recommendation.

Conditioner

Dogs with long coats may need a conditioner to help remove tangles. As with shampoos, your vet can recommend a brand that is right for your dog.

Scissors

Blunt-nosed scissors are handy for trimming the excess fur on your dog's feet, legs, tail, or anal region, as well as for trimming his whiskers.

Grooming the Short Coat

There are two varieties of Chihuahuas: short coats and long coats. Thus, there are two approaches to the grooming of Chihuahuas, depending upon the length of the coat.

Regardless of the variety, the first and foremost requirement in the care of any dog is to keep him in good condition. A dog in good condition is healthy, and a healthy dog's coat is easy to care for. If the dog is not in good coat condition, your grooming is of little value. Proper feeding and exercising are two key ingredients in any conditioning program.

In preparing your short-coat Chihuahua for a show, he will need some trimming. The hair over the eyes should be trimmed, as should the whiskers and long hairs inside the ears and a few stray hairs that may be on the stomach. Round-tipped scissors should be used to reduce the danger of injuring the eyes. A few short-coat Chihuahuas have long hair (called pants) on their hindquarters. When these appear too long and rough, they should be trimmed to give the show dog a neat appearance. The Chihuahua who is a pet, not a show entrant, won't require any such trimming.

Grooming the Long Coat

The long-coat Chihuahua is somewhat different from other long-coat dogs. In certain breeds, the color plays a part in the texture of the coat, but this is not true with the long-coat Chihuahua. The baby coat that they attain when only a few weeks old is a very fluffy, thick coat. They start to lose this when they are four months

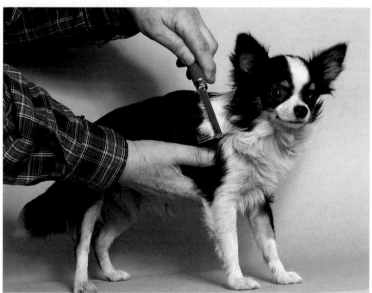

A long-coat Chihuahua should have a coat that is soft and fine, with a graceful appearance.

of age. After they have attained their full coat, they will never be completely "out of coat," with the exception of the time after a bitch whelps, or unless they are neglected.

It is unwise to leave long-coat Chihuahuas outside for a lengthy period of time during very hot weather, as exposure to sun and heat will dry the coat, cause the hair to become brittle, break, streak, and fade.

The long coats do have some undercoat, some more than others, but they should never have a heavy undercoat that would make the hair stand out like that of a Pomeranian. The coat should be soft and fine, with

The long-coat Chihuahua's hair is easily cared for, with minimal trimming required.

a graceful appearance. Their ears and pants should be fringed, and they should have a full tail. The long-coat Chihuahua's hair is easily cared for and requires less brushing than most long-coat breeds.

There is not much trimming necessary on the long-coat Chihuahua in preparation for the show ring. Their nails should be trimmed the same as the short coat. Some people trim the whiskers and others do not. Of course, a bath before going to the show and a good brushing before you go into the ring are suggested.

Brushing

It is worth the investment to obtain a good natural bristle brush. This type of brush is best for all Chihuahua coats in that it will not tear the long hair and offers good massage to the skin of the shorter coats.

Bathing

A Chihuahua needs very few baths if regularly brushed. Too much bathing removes the coat's natural oils, which can lead to dry and itching skin. When a bath is necessary, it is best to use the highest quality shampoo made for dogs, and it should be properly pH-balanced for canine hair and skin.

Cotton should be placed in each ear to avoid water entering the ear canal, and a tiny amount of petroleum jelly can be applied to the rim of each eye to help keep shampoo out. Use lukewarm (never hot) water, and thoroughly massage soap into the coat.

Use a spray hose with a gentle spray to wet the coat and remove all traces of shampoo after the bath. It is extremely important to rinse well with the spray hose because any soap residue allowed to remain in the Chihuahua's coat can lead to dry skin.

Towel dry thoroughly after the bath, and be sure to keep your Chihuahua warm and out of drafts until he is completely dry. All dogs seem to take particular delight in rolling in the grass (or even worse, in something with an offensive smell) immediately after a bath.

Ear Cleaning

Always check ears during grooming sessions to make sure they have no odor and do not appear dry along the edges. In case of odor or wax in the ear, use a cotton swab dipped in rubbing alcohol and wrung out thoroughly. Never probe deeper into the ear than you can see. If odors are very unpleasant, it is best to consult your

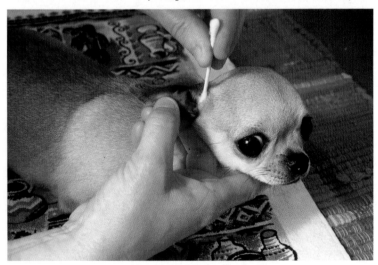

When cleaning your Chihuahua's ears with a cotton swab, never probe deeper than you can see.

veterinarian. If ear edges appear dry, massage them thoroughly with a little coconut or baby oil.

Coat Trimming

There is no clipping or shaving necessary for a Chihuahua. However, if a long-coat Chihuahua's feet grow an excessive amount of hair, they can track in mud or dirt from the outdoors. If this is the case, a good pair of barber's shears can quickly neaten up the foot.

Nail Trimming

Puppyhood is a good time to accustom your Chihuahua to having his nails trimmed and his feet inspected. Always inspect your dog's feet for cracked pads. If your Chihuahua is allowed out in the yard or accompanies you to the park or woods, check between the toes for splinters and thorns. Pay particular attention to any swollen or tender areas. In many sections of the country there is a weed called a "fox tail" that releases a small barbed hook that carries its seed. This hook easily finds its way into a dog's foot or between his toes and very quickly works its way deep into the dog's flesh. Soreness and infection will result soon thereafter. Your veterinarian should remove these barbs before serious problems result.

The nails of a Chihuahua who spends most of his time indoors or on grass when outdoors can grow long very quickly. Do not allow the nails to become overgrown and then expect to cut them back easily. Each nail has a blood vessel called the "quick" running through the center. The quick grows close to the end of the nail and contains very sensitive nerve endings. If the nail is allowed to grow too long, it will be impossible to cut it back to a proper length without cutting into the quick. This causes severe pain to the dog and can also result in a great deal of bleeding that can be very difficult to stop.

Should the quick be nipped in the trimming process, there are a number of blood-clotting products available at pet shops that will almost immediately stem the flow of blood. It is wise to have one of these products on hand in case there is a nail trimming accident or the dog tears a nail on his own.

EXERCISE

A well-balanced diet and regular medical attention from a

Use nail trimming time as an opportunity to inspect your Chihuahua's feet for any abnormalities.

qualified veterinarian are essential in promoting your dog's good health, but so is daily exercise. This keeps him fit and mentally alert. Dogs who have been confined all day while their owners are at work or school need special attention. There should be some time set aside each day for play, as well as for walks after each meal so that they can relieve themselves.

Whenever possible, take a stroll to an empty lot, a playground, or a nearby park. Attach a long lead to your dog's collar. This will help him burn calories, keep trim, and relieve tension and stress that may have had a chance to develop while you were away all day. For people who work during the week, weekend jaunts can be especially beneficial, because you have more time to spend with your canine friend. Games and fun are very important, too, not only for your dog's well-being, but also as a means of creating a strong bond between dogs and owners. You might want to engage your dog in a simple game of fetch with a stick or a rubber ball. Teaching him basic tricks such as rolling over, standing on his hindlegs, or jumping up (all of which can be done inside the home as well) can provide additional exercise. Some dog owners jog with their dogs or take them along on bicycle excursions. Never push your dog too hard; regular extensive training should only be done with adult dogs, never puppies. You should also work up to maximum speed very slowly, working in short time intervals at first, then building up the length of the workouts as your dog improves his condition.

At the very least, however, play with your dog every day to keep him in good shape, physically and mentally. Don't neglect your pet and leave him confined for long periods without giving him attention or time for exercise.

If your own exercise proclivities lie closer to a walk around the block than to 10-mile marathon runs, your choice of a Chihuahua was probably a wise one. The Chihuahua is not a breed that requires taking your energy level to its outer limits. In fact, Chihuahuas will self-exercise if they are allowed the freedom in the house to do so. A Chihuahua is always ready for a romp or even to invent some new game that entails plenty of aerobic activity.

This does not mean that your Chihuahua won't benefit from a daily walk around the block. On the contrary, slow, steady exercise that keeps your companion's heart rate in the working area will do nothing but extend his life. If your Chihuahua is doing all of this with you at his side, you are increasing the chances that the two of you will enjoy each other's company for many more years to come.

Naturally, common sense must be used when determining the extent and the intensity of the exercise you give your Chihuahua. A fast walk for you can mean a full-tilt gallop for your Chihuahua. Remember, young puppies have short bursts of energy and then require long rest periods. No puppy of any breed should be forced to accompany you on extended walks. Serious injuries can result. Again, you should provide short exercise periods and long rest stops for any Chihuahua less than 10 or 12 months of age.

Hot Weather

Caution must be exercised in hot weather. If you are going to take walks, plan to go first thing in the morning if at all possible. If you cannot arrange to do this, wait until the sun has set and the outdoor temperature has dropped to a comfortable degree.

You must never leave your Chihuahua in a car in hot weather. Temperatures can soar in a matter of minutes, and your dog can die of heat exhaustion in less time than you would ever imagine. Rolling down the windows helps little and is dangerous in that an overheated Chihuahua may panic and could attempt to escape through the open window. A word to the wise—leave your dog at home in a cool room on hot days.

Cold Weather

The Chihuahua should not be expected to endure extremely cold weather, either. It is a single-coated breed, and this kind of coat offers little insulation against freezing temperatures. If you are going to be outdoors for any length of time during very cold weather, you may want to consider getting your dog a small coat or jacket, which are available at most pet shops and dog shows.

Do not allow your Chihuahua to remain wet if the two of you get caught in the rain. Thoroughly towel dry the wet Chihuahua as soon as possible in cold or damp weather.

SOCIALIZATION

The Chihuahua is by nature a happy dog who takes most situations in stride; it is important, though, to accommodate the breed's natural instincts by making sure your dog is accustomed to all kinds of everyday events. Traffic, strange noises, loud or hyperactive children, and strange animals can be very intimidating to a dog of any breed who has never experienced them before. Gently and gradually introduce your puppy to as many strange situations as you possibly can.

Make it a practice to take your Chihuahua with you whenever practical. The breed is a real crowd pleaser, and you will find your Chihuahua will savor all the attention he gets.

TRAINING Your Chihuahua

T here is no breed of dog that cannot be trained, although it does appear that getting the desired response from some breeds is more difficult than others. In many cases, however, this has more to do with the trainer and his or her training methods than with the dog's inability to learn. With the proper approach, any dog who is not mentally deficient can be taught to be a good canine citizen. Many dog owners do not understand how a dog learns, and they also don't realize they can be breed-specific in their approach to training.

Young puppies have an amazing capacity to learn, and this capacity is greater than most humans realize. It is important to remember, though, that these young puppies also forget with great speed unless they are reminded of what they have learned by continual reinforcement.

As puppies leave the nest, they began their search for two things: a pack leader and rules that the leader has established. Because puppies, particularly Chihuahua puppies, are cute and very small, their owners sometimes fail to supply the very basic needs of their dogs. Instead, they immediately begin to respond to the demands of the puppy. For example, a puppy may quickly learn that he will be allowed into the house or a room because he is barking or whining, not because he can only enter a room when he is not barking or whining.

Chihuahuas are highly trainable dogs, and they are capable of learning a variety of tasks.

Instead of learning that the only way he will be fed is to follow a set procedure (i.e., sitting or lying down on command), he may learn that leaping about the kitchen or barking incessantly is what gets results.

If a young puppy cannot find a pack leader in his owner, the puppy will assume the role of pack leader himself. Yes, even though he is very small, the Chihuahua puppy will learn to make his own rules if there are no rules imposed. Unfortunately, the negligent owner will continually reinforce the puppy's decisions by allowing him to govern the household. With small dogs like the Chihuahua, this scenario can produce chaos; with large dogs, the situation can be downright dangerous. Neither situation is acceptable.

The key to successful training lies in establishing the proper relationship between dog and owner. The owner or the family must be the pack leader, and the individual or family must provide the rules by which the dog abides. Once this is established, ease of training depends in great part upon just how much a dog depends on his owner's approval. The entirely dependent dog lives to please his master and will do everything in his power to evoke the approval response from the person to whom he is devoted. At the opposite end of the pole is the totally independent dog who is not remotely concerned with what his owner thinks or wants. Dependency varies from one breed to the next, and to a degree, within breeds as well. Chihuahuas are no exception to this rule. Fortunately for Chihuahua owners, however, the breed really wants to please.

HOUSETRAINING

Housetraining a Chihuahua is no more difficult than training any other breed of dog. The problem, however, lies in the fact that the breed's accidents are so small that they can be hard to see, and a Chihuahua can establish bad habits before they are even noticed. Therefore, constant vigilance is extremely important.

A major key to successfully training your Chihuahua, whether it be obedience training or housetraining, is avoidance. It is much easier for your Chihuahua to learn something if you do not first have to have him unlearn some bad habit. The crate training method of housetraining is a highly successful method of preventing bad habits before they begin.

First-time dog owners are initially inclined to see the crate method of housetraining as cruel, but those same people usually

Teaching your Chihuahua puppy to eliminate in a certain area of the yard will help him become housetrained.

change their minds after observing how it really works. They are also surprised to find that their puppy will eventually come to think of his crate as a place of private retreat—a den to which he will retreat for rest and privacy. The success of the crate method is based upon the fact that puppies will not soil the area in which they sleep.

Use of a crate reduces housetraining time to an absolute minimum and avoids keeping a puppy under constant stress by incessantly correcting him for making mistakes in the house. The anti-crate advocates consider it cruel to confine a puppy for a length of time but find no problem in constantly harassing the puppy because he has eliminated on the carpet and behind the sofa.

Crates come in a wide variety of styles. The fiberglass shipping kennels that airlines use are popular with many Chihuahua owners, but residents of extremely warm climates sometimes prefer the wire cage type. Both are available at pet stores. Another type of crate, the Nylabone® Fold-Away Pet Carrier, is a great space-saving crate. When your pet is not using the crate, it can be folded down and stored away. It's ideal for use in apartments and is perfect for travel.

The crate used for housetraining should only be large enough for the puppy to comfortably stand up, lie down, and stretch out. There are many sizes from which to choose, but a small crate is the ideal size for most Chihuahuas.

A crate, such as the Nylabone® Fold-Away Pet Carrier, is an effective housetraining tool.

Begin using the crate as a place to feed your puppy. Keep the door closed and latched while the puppy is eating. When the meal is finished, open the cage and carry your puppy outdoors or to the spot where you want him to learn to eliminate. In the event you do not have access to or do not wish to use the outdoors, begin housetraining by placing newspapers in some out-of-the-way corner that is easily accessible to the puppy. If you consistently take your puppy to the same spot, you will reinforce the habit of going there for that purpose.

It is important that you do not let the puppy loose after eating. Young puppies will eliminate almost immediately after eating or drinking. They will also be ready to relieve themselves when they first wake up and after playtime. If you keep a watchful eye on your Chihuahua, you will quickly learn the telltale signs that he needs to go out. A puppy usually circles and sniffs the floor just before he relieves himself. Do not give your puppy an opportunity to learn that he can eliminate in the house! Your housetraining chores will be reduced considerably if you avoid this problem in the first place.

If you are not able to watch your puppy every minute, he should be in his crate with the door securely latched. Each time you put your puppy in the crate, give him a small treat of some kind. Throw the treat to the back of the crate and encourage the puppy to walk in on his own. When he does so, praise him and perhaps hand him another treat through the opening in the front of the crate.

Do not succumb to your puppy's complaints about being in his crate. The puppy must learn to stay there and do so without unnecessary complaining. A quick "no" command and a tap on the crate will usually get the puppy to understand that his theatrics will not result in liberation. (Remember, you—the pack leader—make the rules, and the puppy seeks to learn what they are!)

You have to remember that a puppy of 8 to 12 weeks will not be able to contain himself for very long. Except at night, puppies of that age must relieve themselves every few hours. Your schedule must be adjusted accordingly. Also make sure that your puppy has relieved himself—both bowel and bladder—the last thing at night, and do not dawdle when you wake up in the morning.

Your first priority in the morning is to get your puppy outdoors. Just how early this ritual takes place will depend much more on your puppy than on you. If your Chihuahua puppy is like other puppies, there will be no doubt in your mind when he needs to be let out.

You will also very quickly learn to tell the difference between the "this is an emergency" complaint and the "I just want out" grumbling. However, do not test the young puppy's ability to contain himself. His vocal demand to be let out is confirmation that the housetraining lesson is being learned.

Should you find it necessary to be away from home all day, you will not be able to leave your puppy in a crate. However, do not make the mistake of allowing him to roam the house or even a large room at will. Confine the puppy to a very small room or partitioned-off area, and cover the floor with newspaper. Make this area large enough so that the puppy will not have to relieve himself next to his bed, food, or water bowls. You will soon find that he will be inclined to use one particular spot to perform his bowel and bladder functions. When you are home, you must take the puppy to this exact spot to eliminate at the appropriate time.

BASIC TRAINING

Where you are emotionally and the environment in which you train are just as important to your dog's training as his state of mind at the time. Never begin training when you are irritated, distressed, or preoccupied. You should also never begin basic training in a place that interferes with you or your dog's concentration. Once the commands are understood and learned, you can begin testing your dog in public places, but the two of you should first work in a place where you can fully concentrate on each other.

You must remain aware of the sensitivity level of your Chihuahua and his desire to please. Chihuahuas respond well to lots of praise, but they do not respond to yelling or harsh discipline. Never resort to shaking or striking your puppy. A very stern "no!" is usually more than sufficient, and even when dealing with the most persistent unwanted behavior, striking the ground with a rolled-up newspaper is about as extreme as you will ever need to be.

The extent to which the breed can be trained knows few limits. Do not feel limited by the diminutive size of the Chihuahua. The breed's ability to learn and perform far exceeds its size, and the breed has done amazingly well in the area of both obedience trials and tracking events.

Leash Training

Begin leash training by putting a soft, lightweight collar on your puppy. After a few hours of occasional scratching at the unaccustomed addition, your puppy will quickly forget it is even there.

It may not be necessary for the puppy or adult Chihuahua to wear his collar and identification tags within the confines of your home, but no Chihuahua should ever leave home—even if you plan to carry the dog—without a collar and the attached leash held securely in your hand.

Begin getting your puppy accustomed to his collar by leaving it on for a few minutes at a time. Gradually extend the time you leave the collar on. Once this is accomplished, attach a very lightweight leash to the collar while you are playing with the puppy. Do not try to guide the puppy at first. You are only trying to get the puppy used to having something attached to the collar.

Get your puppy to follow you as you move around by coaxing him along with a treat of some kind. Let the puppy smell what you have in your hand and then move a few steps back, holding the treat in front of the puppy's nose. Just as soon as the puppy takes a few steps toward you, praise him enthusiastically and continue to do so as you move along.

Make the first few lessons brief and fun for the puppy. Continue the lessons in your home or yard until the puppy is completely unconcerned about the fact that he is on a leash. With a treat in one

Keep initial leash training lessons short in duration, and gradually work up to longer sessions.

hand and the leash in the other, you can begin to use both to guide the puppy in the direction you wish to go. Eventually, the two of you can venture out on the sidewalk in front of your house and then on to adventures everywhere! This is one lesson no puppy is too young to learn.

"No"

One of the most important commands your Chihuahua puppy will ever learn is the meaning of the word "no." It is critical that the puppy learn this command as soon as possible. One important piece of advice in using this and all other commands is to never give a command that you are not prepared and able to enforce. A good leader does not enforce rules arbitrarily. The only way a puppy learns to obey commands is to realize that once issued, commands must be complied with. Learning the no command should start on the first day of the puppy's arrival in your home.

Be fair to your dog. While he can easily learn the difference between things he can and cannot do, a dog is not able to learn that there are some things he can do sometimes but not others. For example, yelling at your dog for lying on the sofa today when it was perfectly acceptable for him to do so the previous day will only confuse him.

Come

The next important lesson for the Chihuahua puppy to learn is to come when called; therefore, it is very important that your puppy learn his name as soon as possible. Constant repetition is what works when teaching a puppy his name. Use the name every time you talk to your puppy. Talk to your dog? There is a quotation I particularly like that appeared in an old British dog book I found regarding conversations with our canine friends. It states simply, "Of course you should talk to your dogs. But talk sense!"

Learning to come on command could save your dog's life when the two of you venture out into the world. Your dog must understand that the come command is one that has to be obeyed without question, but he should not associate that command with fear. Your dog's response to his name and the word "come" should always be associated with a pleasant experience, such as great praise and petting or even a food treat. Remember that it is much easier to avoid the establishment of bad habits than it is to correct them

Use words of praise and a treat when your Chihuahua successfully completes a training lesson.

once entrenched. Never give the come command unless you are sure your puppy will come to you.

The very young Chihuahua puppy will normally want to stay as close to his owner as possible, especially in strange surroundings. When your puppy sees you moving away, his natural inclination will be to get close to you. This is a perfect time to use the come command. Also, the very young puppy is far more inclined to respond to the come command than the older dog. Young puppies are entirely dependent upon you. An older dog may lose some of that dependency and become preoccupied with his surroundings, so start your come command training early.

Use the command initially when the puppy is already on his way to you, or give the command while walking or running away from the youngster. Clap your hands and sound very happy and excited about having the puppy join in on this game. You may want to attach a long leash of some very lightweight material to the puppy's collar to ensure the correct response. Do not chase or punish your puppy for not obeying the come command. Doing so in the initial

Only very light, extremely gentle pressure should be applied to help your Chihuahua learn to sit.

stages of training will make the puppy associate the command with something to fear, which will result in avoidance rather than the immediate positive response you desire. It is imperative that you praise your puppy and give him a treat when he does come to you, even if he voluntarily delays responding for many minutes.

Sit

The sit and stay commands are just as important to your Chihuahua puppy's safety as the no command and learning to come when called. Even very young Chihuahuas can learn the sit command quickly, especially if it appears to be a game and a food treat is involved.

First, remember that the Chihuahua-in-training should always be on a collar and leash for all of his lessons. A Chihuahua puppy is curious about everything that goes on around him, and a puppy is not beyond getting up and scurrying away when he has decided that he needs to investigate something.

With the treat in your hand, raise it above the dog's head while commanding him to sit until he is in the correct position. A food treat of some kind always seems to make the experience that much more enjoyable for the puppy.

Of course, as in anything you do with your Chihuahua, good sense must be used in the amount of physical pressure you apply to get a desired response. Never push down quickly or with too much force. If need be, you may have to "help" the hind legs slide forward and down with your other hand.

Continue holding your dog in the sit position and repeat the sit command several times. If your puppy makes an attempt to get up, repeat the command yet again until the correct position is assumed. Make your puppy stay in this position a little bit longer with each lesson. Begin with a few seconds, and increase the time as lessons progress over the following weeks.

If your puppy attempts to get up or lie down, he should be corrected by simply saying, "Sit!" in a firm voice. This should be accompanied by returning the dog to the desired position. Only when you decide that your dog may get up should he do so. Do not test the extent of your young Chihuahua puppy's patience. Remember, you are dealing with a baby, and the attention span of any youngster is relatively limited. When you do decide the dog can get up, call his name, say, "Okay," and make a big fuss over him.

Praise and a food treat are in order each time your puppy responds correctly.

Stay

Once your puppy has mastered the sit lesson, you may start on the stay command. With your Chihuahua on leash and facing you, command him to sit and take a step or two back. Firmly say, "Sit, stay!" if your dog attempts to get up to follow. While you are saying this, raise your hand, palm toward the dog, and again command, "Stay!"

If your dog attempts to get up, you must correct him at once, returning him to the sit position and repeating, "Stay!" Once your Chihuahua begins to understand what you want, you can gradually increase the distance you step back. With a long leash attached to your dog's collar, start with a few steps and gradually increase the distance to several yards. It is important for your puppy to learn that the sit and stay commands must be obeyed no matter how far away you are. With advanced training, your Chihuahua can be taught that the command is to be obeyed even when you leave the room or are entirely out of sight.

As your Chihuahua becomes accustomed to responding to this lesson and is able to remain in the sit position for as long as you command, do not end the command by calling the dog to you. Walk back to your puppy and say, "Okay." This will let your dog know that the command is over. Once your Chihuahua becomes entirely dependable in this lesson, you can then call the dog to you.

The sit and stay commands can take considerable time and patience to teach puppies. Because their attention spans will be short, it's important to keep the stay part of the lesson very brief until your puppy is about six months old.

Down

When you feel confident that your puppy is comfortable with the sit and stay commands, you can start work on down. Down is the single word command for lie down. Use the down command only when you want the dog to lie down. If you want your Chihuahua to stop jumping up on people, use the off command. Do not interchange these two commands. Doing so will only serve to confuse your dog, and evoking the desired response will become next to impossible.

Begin teaching your Chihuahua the down after he has mastered the sit and stay commands.

The down position is especially useful if you want your Chihuahua to remain in one place for a long period of time. Most dogs are far more inclined to stay put when lying down than when they are sitting or standing. Teaching your Chihuahua the down may take more time and patience than the previous lessons the two of you have undertaken. Some animal behaviorists believe that assuming the down position somehow represents greater submissiveness.

With your Chihuahua sitting in front of and facing you, hold a treat in your right hand, with the excess part of the leash in your left hand. Hold the treat under your dog's nose and slowly bring your hand down to the ground. Your dog will follow the treat with his head and neck. As he does this, give the command, "Down," and exert *light* pressure on the dog's shoulders with your left hand. If your dog resists the pressure on his shoulders, do not continue pushing down. Doing so will only create more resistance. Reach down and slide the dog's feet toward you until he is lying down.

An alternative method of getting your Chihuahua into the down position is to move around the dog's right side. As you draw his

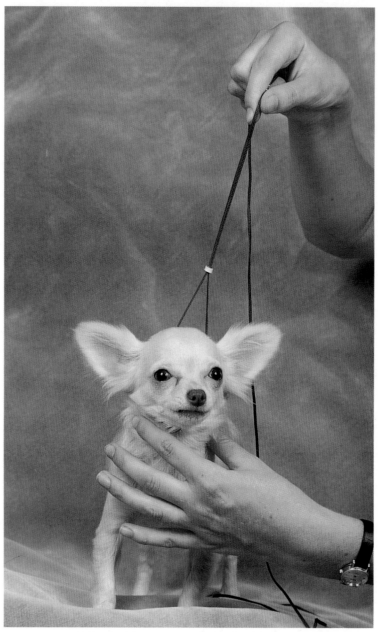

Training your Chihuahua to participate in advanced activities, like showing, is a time-consuming but ultimately rewarding task.

attention downward with your right hand, slide your left hand under the dog's front legs and gently slide them forward. You will undoubtedly have to be on your knees next to the dog in order to do this.

As your dog's forelegs begin to slide out to his front, keep moving the treat along the ground while continually repeating, "Down" until his whole body is lying on the ground. Once your dog has assumed the position you desire, give him the treat and lots of praise. Continue assisting your Chihuahua into the down position until he does so on his own. Be firm and be patient.

Heel

In learning to heel, your Chihuahua will walk on your left side with his shoulder near your leg no matter what direction you might go or how quickly you turn. Learning this command can be an extremely valuable lesson for your dog. A Chihuahua who darts back and forth in front of or under his owner's feet can endanger himself and could cause serious injury for his owner as well.

Teaching your Chihuahua to heel is critical to off-leash control and will not only make your daily walks far more enjoyable, it will make a far more tractable companion when the two of you are in crowded or confusing situations. I do not recommend ever allowing your Chihuahua to be off leash when you are away from home, but it is important to know you can control your dog no matter what the circumstances are.

A lightweight collar or a small jeweler's snake chain is best for training toy dogs, especially for the heeling lesson. Changing from the collar your dog regularly wears to something different indicates what you are doing is "business" and not just a casual stroll. The pet shop where you purchase your other supplies can assist you in selecting the best training collar to help you with your lessons.

As you train your Chihuahua puppy to walk along on the leash, you should accustom the youngster to walk on your left side. The leash should cross your body from the dog's collar to your right hand. The excess portion of the leash will be folded into your right hand, and your left hand will be used to make corrections with the leash. A quick, very gentle tug on the leash with your left hand will keep your dog from lunging from side to side, pulling ahead, or darting between your legs. As you make a correction, give the heel command. Keep the leash loose when your dog maintains the proper position at your side. If your dog begins to drift away, give the leash a soft tug and guide the dog back to the correct position. Give the heel command again. Do not pull on the lead with steady pressure. What is needed is a quick but gentle tugging motion to get your dog's attention.

ADVANCED TRAINING AND ACTIVITIES

There is no end to the number of activities that you and your Chihuahua can enjoy together. The breed is highly successful in both conformation shows and obedience trials. There are Canine Good Citizen® certificates that can be earned through the AKC; many owners enjoy helping their dog to earn these certificates, and the experience serves to make a good companion even better.

Therapy Dogs

Owners not inclined toward competitive events might find enjoyment in having their Chihuahuas serve as therapy dogs. There is nothing more rewarding than seeing someone else get as much

happiness and delight out of your dog as you do, and there are some dogs who just seem to love getting a smile out of anyone and everyone. Getting involved with therapy work is a wonderful way to spread the joy of dog ownership to those who may most benefit from it. Statistics show that this aspect of health care is making a real impact and creating some remarkable results with the sick, the elderly, and people with special needs. If your dog has a particularly even and friendly temperament, therapy work may be perfect for him and especially rewarding for you.

Both you and your Chihuahua will benefit from participation in therapy or assistance work.

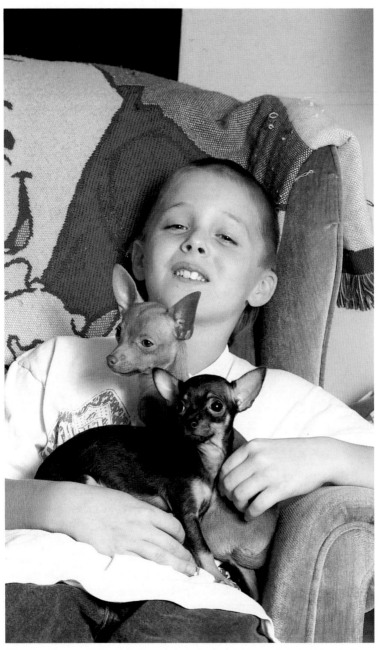

Therapy dogs are highly trained companions who serve to enrich the lives of others.

You can have your Chihuahua visit the elderly in nursing homes or patients in hospitals, or you can enroll him in a program that helps educate children about the care and training of dogs. If you contact therapy programs or your local humane society, they can better inform you of programs in your area and the best way to get your dog started. When your dog becomes a therapy dog, he is doing more than enriching your life—he is making a valuable contribution to the quality of the life of others.

Assistance Dogs

Some dogs can be trained to assist people who have physical disabilities. They can help the blind get around independently, aid the deaf in hearing the telephone or the doorbell, and assist those confined to wheelchairs to accomplish everyday activities, like opening doors or fetching things they need. There are special programs that train and screen these puppies, and some also offer foster programs for people who can take in puppies and train and socialize them until they are ready to be placed with that special person.

Chihuahuas are also wonderful dogs to use in elementary school programs to teach responsible pet care. The size of the breed does not intimidate even the shyest child. Dogs who visit schools can also be taught an endless array of tricks that will keep children entertained for hours.

The well-trained Chihuahua can provide a whole world of activities for the owner. You are limited only by the amount of time you wish to invest in this remarkable breed.

TRAINING CLASSES

There are few limits to what a patient, consistent Chihuahua owner can teach his or her dog. Chihuahuas are highly trainable. Remember the breed's lifelong history of companionship and desire to please. Once lessons are mastered, you will find that most Chihuahuas will perform with enough enthusiasm and gusto to make all the hard work worthwhile.

For advanced obedience work beyond the basics, it is wise for the Chihuahua owner to consider local professional assistance. Professional trainers have long-standing experience in avoiding the pitfalls of obedience training, and they can help you to avoid them as well.

This training assistance can be obtained in many ways. Classes are particularly good in that your dog will learn to obey commands

For advanced obedience work beyond the basics, local professional assistance may be a viable option.

in spite of all the interesting sights and smells of other dogs. There are free-of-charge classes at many parks and recreation facilities, as well as very formal and sometimes very expensive individual lessons with private trainers. There are also some obedience schools that will take your Chihuahua and train him for you. However, unless your schedule provides no time at all to train your dog, having someone else train the dog for you would be last on my list of recommendations. The rapport that develops between owner and dog in this situation is incomparable. The effort you expend to teach your dog to be a pleasant companion and good canine citizen will pay off in years of enjoyable companionship.

DENTAL CARE for Your Chihuahua

Y ou have a new puppy! Anyone who has ever raised a puppy is abundantly aware of how this new arrival affects the household. Your puppy will chew anything he can reach, chase your shoelaces, and play "tear the rag" with any piece of clothing he can find.

When puppies are newly born, they have no teeth. At about four weeks of age, puppies of most breeds begin to develop their deciduous (baby) teeth. They begin eating semi-solid food, biting and fighting with their littermates, and learning discipline from their mother. As their new teeth come in, they inflict pain on their mother's breasts, so feeding sessions become less frequent and shorter in duration. By six or eight weeks, the mother will start growling to warn her pups when they are fighting too roughly or hurting her as they nurse too much with their new teeth.

CHEWING

Puppies need to chew, as it is a necessary part of their physical and mental development. They develop muscles and necessary life skills

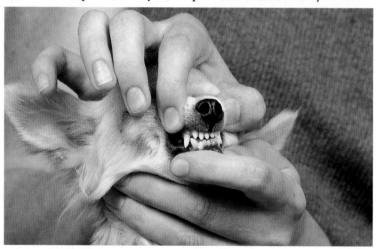

Regular dental examinations performed by a veterinarian will help your Chihuahua's teeth remain healthy.

Examine your dog's mouth weekly throughout his first year to check for any potential problems.

as they drag objects around, fight over possessions, and vocalize alerts and warnings. Puppies chew on things to explore their world. They are using their sense of taste to determine what is food and what is not. How else can they tell an electrical cord from a lizard?

At about four months of age, most puppies begin shedding their baby teeth. Often, these teeth need some help to come out to make way for the permanent teeth. The incisors (front teeth) will be replaced first. Then, the adult canine or fang teeth erupt. When a baby tooth is not shed before the permanent tooth comes in, veterinarians call it a retained deciduous tooth. This condition will often cause gum infections by trapping hair and debris between the permanent tooth and the retained baby tooth. Puppies who are given adequate chew toys will exhibit less destructive behavior, develop more physically, and have less chance of retained deciduous teeth.

VISITING THE VET

During the first year, your veterinarian should see your dog at regular intervals. Your vet will let you know when to bring your puppy in for vaccinations and parasite examinations. At each visit, your vet should inspect the lips, teeth, and mouth as part of a complete physical examination.

You should also take some part in the maintenance of your dog's oral health. Examine your dog's mouth weekly throughout his first year to make sure there are no sores, foreign objects, tooth problems,

Chewing is a necessary part of your Chihuahua puppy's mental and physical development.

Statistics show that puppies who are given adequate chew toys will exhibit less destructive behavior.

etc. If your dog drools excessively, shakes his head, or has bad breath, consult your veterinarian. By the time your dog is six months old, his permanent teeth are all in, and plaque can start to accumulate on the tooth surfaces. This is when your dog needs good dental-care habits to prevent buildup on his teeth.

Brushing is best—that is a fact that cannot be denied. However, some dogs do not like their teeth brushed regularly, or you may not be able to accomplish the task. In this case, you should consider a product that will help prevent plaque buildup, such as a Nylabone®.

PERIODONTAL DISEASE

By the time dogs are four years old, 75 percent of them have some type of periodontal disease; it is the most common infection in dogs. Yearly examinations by your vet are essential to maintaining your dog's good health. If periodontal disease is detected, he or she may recommend a prophylactic cleaning. To do a thorough cleaning, it will be necessary to put your dog under anesthesia.

With modern gas anesthetics and monitoring equipment, the procedure is fairly safe. Your veterinarian will scale the teeth with an ultrasound scaler or hand instrument. This removes the calculus from the teeth. If there are calculus deposits below the gum line, the veterinarian will plane the roots to make them smooth. After all of the calculus has been removed, the teeth are polished with pumice in a polishing cup. If any medical or surgical treatment is needed, it is done at this time. The final step would be fluoride treatment and your follow-up treatment at home. If the periodontal disease is advanced, the veterinarian may prescribe a medicated mouth rinse or antibiotics for use at home. Make sure your dog has safe, clean, and attractive chew toys, like Nylabones®, and healthy treats.

Maintaining Oral Health

As your dog ages, professional examinations and cleanings should become more frequent. The mouth should be inspected at least once a year. Your vet may recommend visits every six months. In the geriatric patient, organs such as the heart, liver, and kidneys do not function as well as they did when your dog was young. Your vet will probably want to test these organs' functions prior to using general anesthesia for dental cleaning.

If your dog is a good chewer and you work closely with your vet, he can keep all of his teeth all of his life. However, as your dog ages, his sense of smell, sight, and taste will diminish. He may not have the desire to chase, trap, or chew his toys. He also will not have the energy to chew for long periods, as arthritis and periodontal disease could make chewing painful. This will leave you with more responsibility for keeping his teeth clean and healthy. However, the dog who would not let you brush his teeth at one year of age may let you brush his teeth now that he is ten years old.

If you train your dog with good chewing habits as a puppy, he will have healthier teeth throughout his life.

HEALTH CARE for Your Chihuahua

Veterinary medicine has become far more sophisticated than what it was in the past. This can be attributed to the increase in household pets, and consequently, the demand for better care for them. Also, human medicine has become far more complex. Today, diagnostic testing in veterinary medicine parallels human diagnostics. Because of better technology, we can expect our pets to live healthier lives, thereby increasing their life spans.

PHYSICAL EXAMS

During a physical exam, your veterinarian will check your pet's overall condition, which includes listening to the heart; checking the respiration; feeling the abdomen, muscles, and joints; checking the mouth, which includes looking at gum color and checking for signs of gum disease, along with plaque buildup; checking the ears

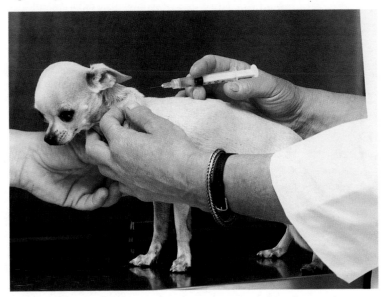

Your veterinarian will vaccinate your Chihuahua to guard against various canine diseases.

for signs of an infection or ear mites; examining the eyes; and last but not least, checking the condition of the skin and coat.

The veterinarian should ask you questions regarding your pet's eating and elimination habits and invite you to relay your questions. It is a good idea to prepare a list so as not to forget anything. He or she should discuss the proper diet and the quantity to feed your pet. If this differs from your breeder's recommendation, you should convey to him or her what the breeder's choice is and see if he or she approves. If he or she recommends changing the diet, this should be done over a few days so as not to cause your dog gastrointestinal upset.

It is customary to take in a fresh stool sample (just a small amount) to test for intestinal parasites. It must be fresh, preferably within 12 hours, because the eggs hatch quickly and after hatching will not be able to be observed under the microscope. If your pet isn't obliging, the technician can usually take a sample in the clinic.

The First Checkup

You will want to take your new puppy or dog in for his first checkup within 48 to 72 hours after acquiring him. Many breeders strongly recommend this checkup, as do humane shelters. This is

Your new puppy should be taken to the vet for a checkup within 48 to 72 hours of acquiring him.

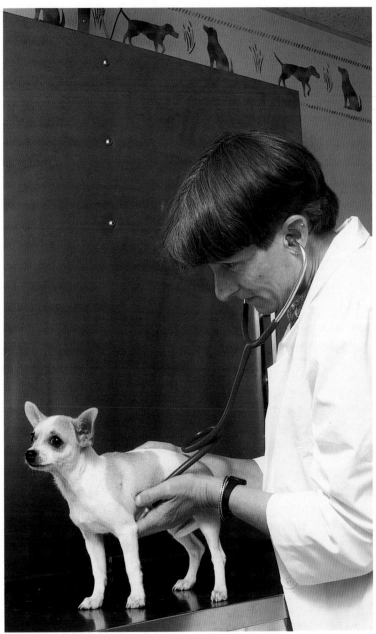

A physical examination will include an evaluation of your Chihuahua's overall condition.

because a dog can appear healthy, but he may have a serious problem that is not apparent to the layman. Most pets have some type of minor flaw that may never cause a real problem.

This first checkup is a good time to establish a relationship with your veterinarian and to learn the office policy regarding its hours and how the staff handles emergencies. Usually, the breeder or another conscientious pet owner is a good reference for locating a capable veterinarian. You should be aware that not all vets give the same quality of service. You should not make your selection based on the least expensive clinic, as you may be shortchanging your pet. There is also the possibility that the least expensive clinic might eventually cost you more due to improper diagnosis, treatment, etc.

If you are selecting a new veterinarian, feel free to ask for a tour of the clinic. You should inquire about making an appointment for a tour, because all clinics are working clinics and may not be available all day for sightseers. You may worry less if you see where your pet will be spending the day if he ever needs to be hospitalized.

Immunizations

It is important that you take your dog's vaccination record with you on your first visit. In the case of a puppy, presumably the breeder has seen to the vaccinations up to the time you acquired your pet. Veterinarians differ in their vaccination protocol. It is not unusual for your puppy to have received vaccinations for distemper, hepatitis, leptospirosis, parvovirus, and parainfluenza every two to three weeks from the age of five or six weeks. Usually, this is a combined injection and is typically called the DHLPP.

The DHLPP is given through at least 12 to 14 weeks of age, and it is customary to continue with another parvovirus vaccine at 16 to 18 weeks. You may wonder why so many immunizations are necessary. A puppy inherits antibodies in the womb from his mother, but no one knows for sure when these antibodies actually leave the puppy's body, although it is customarily accepted that distemper antibodies are gone by 12 weeks. Usually, parvovirus antibodies are gone by 16 to 18 weeks of age. However, it is possible for the maternal antibodies to be gone much earlier or even at a later age. Therefore, immunizations are started at an early age. The vaccine will not give immunity, though, as long as maternal antibodies are present.

The rabies vaccination is given at three or six months of age, depending on your local laws. A vaccine for bordetella (kennel cough) is advisable and can be given any time from the age of five weeks. The coronavirus is not commonly given unless there is a problem locally. The Lyme vaccine is necessary in endemic areas. Lyme disease has been reported in 47 states.

After your puppy has completed his puppy vaccinations, you will continue to booster the DHLPP once a year. It is customary to booster the rabies one year after the first vaccine, and then, depending on where you live, the booster should be given every year or every three years, depending on your local laws. The Lyme and corona vaccines are boostered annually, and it is recommended that the bordetella be boostered every six to eight months.

Annual Visit

The annual checkup, which includes booster vaccinations, a check for intestinal parasites, and a test for heartworm, is extremely important. However, make sure to get this checkup from a qualified veterinarian, because more harm than good can come to your dog through improper vaccinations, possibly from inferior vaccines and/or the wrong schedule. It is also important for your veterinarian to know your dog, and this is especially true during middle age and through the geriatric years. Your older dog may require more than one physical a year. The annual physical is good preventive medicine. Through early diagnosis and subsequent treatment, your dog can maintain a longer and better quality of life.

COMMON CANINE DISEASES

Distemper

Distemper is virtually an incurable disease. If the dog recovers, he is subject to severe nervous disorders. The virus attacks every tissue in the body and resembles a bad cold with a fever. It can cause a runny nose and eyes and gastrointestinal disorders, which may lead to a poor appetite, vomiting, and diarrhea. Raccoons, foxes, wolves, mink, and other dogs carry the virus. Unvaccinated youngsters and senior citizens are very susceptible. This is still a common disease.

Hepatitis

Hepatitis is a virus that is most serious in very young dogs. It is spread by contact with an infected animal or its stool or urine. The virus affects the liver and kidneys and is characterized by high fever, depression, and lack of appetite. Recovered animals may be afflicted with chronic illnesses.

Leptospirosis

Leptospirosis is a bacterial disease transmitted by contact with the urine of infected dogs, rats, or other wildlife. It produces severe symptoms of fever, depression, jaundice, and internal bleeding and was fatal before the vaccine was developed. Recovered dogs can be carriers, and the disease can be transmitted from dogs to humans.

Parvovirus

Parvovirus was first noted in the late 1970s and is still a fatal disease. However, with proper vaccinations, early diagnosis, and prompt treatment, it is a manageable disease. It attacks the bone marrow and intestinal tract. Symptoms include depression, loss of appetite, vomiting, diarrhea, and collapse. Immediate medical attention is necessary in order to manage the disease.

Rabies

Rabies is shed in the saliva and is carried by raccoons, skunks, foxes, other dogs, and cats. It attacks nerve tissue, resulting in paralysis and death. Rabies can be transmitted to people and is virtually always fatal. This disease is reappearing in the suburbs.

Bordetella (Kennel Cough)

The symptoms of bordetella are coughing, sneezing, hacking, and retching, accompanied by a nasal discharge usually lasting from a few days to several weeks. There are several disease-producing organisms responsible for this disease. The present vaccines are helpful but do not protect for all of the strains. It is usually not life threatening, but in some instances it can progress to a serious bronchopneumonia. The disease is highly contagious. The vaccination should be given routinely to dogs who come into contact with other dogs through boarding kennels, training classes, or visits to the groomer.

Coronavirus

Coronavirus is usually self-limiting and is not a life-threatening disease. It was first noted in the late 1970s, about a year before parvovirus. The virus produces a yellow/brown stool, and there may be depression, vomiting, and diarrhea.

Lyme Disease

Lyme disease was first diagnosed in the US in 1976 in Lyme, Connecticut, in people who lived in close proximity to the deer tick. The disease is usually spread by these ticks, and symptoms may include acute lameness, fever, swelling of joints, and loss of appetite. Your veterinarian can advise you if you live in an endemic area.

INTESTINAL PARASITES

Intestinal parasites are more prevalent in some areas than others. Climate, soil, and contamination are big factors contributing to the incidence of intestinal parasites. Eggs are passed in the stool, lie on the ground, and then become infective in a certain number of days. Each of the worms described below has a different life cycle. Your dog's best chance of becoming and remaining worm-free is to always keep your yard clean and free of the dog's fecal matter. A fenced-in yard keeps stray dogs out, which is certainly helpful.

Intestinal parasites are more prevalent in some areas than others, and it's important to keep your yard as clean as possible to prevent infestation.

Having a fecal examination performed on your dog twice a year, or more often if there is a problem, is recommended. If your dog has a positive fecal sample, he will be given the appropriate medication, and you will be asked to bring back another stool sample after a certain period of time (depending on the type of worm); then he will be rewormed. This process continues until he has at least two negative samples. Different types of worms require different medications. You will be wasting your money and doing your dog an injustice by buying over-the-counter medications without first consulting your veterinarian.

Hookworms

Hookworms are almost microscopic intestinal worms that can cause anemia and may lead to some serious problems, including death, in young puppies. Hookworms can be transmitted to humans through penetration of the skin. Puppies may be born with them.

Roundworms

Roundworms are spaghetti-like worms that can cause a potbellied appearance and dull coat, along with more severe symptoms such as vomiting, diarrhea, and coughing. Puppies acquire these while in the mother's uterus and through lactation. Both hookworms and roundworms may be acquired through ingestion.

Whipworms

Whipworms have a three-month life cycle and are not acquired through the dam. They cause intermittent diarrhea, usually with mucus. Whipworms are possibly the most difficult worm to eradicate. Their eggs are very resistant to most environmental factors and can last for years until the proper conditions enable them to mature. Whipworms are seldom seen in the stool.

OTHER INTERNAL PARASITES

Coccidiosis and Giardiasis

Coccidiosis and giardiasis, both protozoal infections, usually affect pups, especially in places where large numbers of puppies are brought together. Older dogs may harbor these infections but not show signs unless they are stressed. Symptoms include diarrhea, weight loss, and lack of appetite. These infections are not always apparent in fecal examination.

Tapeworms

Seldom apparent on fecal floatation, tapeworms frequently show up as rice-like segments around the dog's anus and the base of the tail. Tapeworms are long, flat, and ribbon-like, sometimes several feet in length, and made up of many segments about 5/8 of an inch long.

There are two common causes of tapeworm found in dogs. First, the larval form of the flea tapeworm parasite could mature in an intermediate host, the flea, before it can become infective. Your dog may acquire this by ingesting the flea through licking and chewing. Secondly, rabbits, rodents, and certain large game animals serve as intermediate hosts for other species of tapeworms. If your dog eats one of these infected hosts, he can acquire tapeworms.

Heartworms

Heartworms are worms that reside in the heart and adjacent blood vessels of the lung. They produce microfilaria, which circulate in the bloodstream. It is possible for a dog to be infected with any number of these worms, which are 6 to 14 inches long. Heartworm disease is life-threatening and expensive to treat, but it is easily prevented. Depending on where you live, your veterinarian may recommend a preventive year-round and either an annual or semiannual blood test. The most common preventive is given once a month.

External Parasites

Fleas

Fleas are not only a dog's worst enemies, but they are also enemies of the owner's pocketbook. The majority of dogs are allergic to the bite of a flea, and in many cases, it only takes one fleabite to require treatment. The protein in a flea's saliva is the culprit. Allergic dogs have a reaction, which usually results in a "hot spot." More than likely, such a reaction will involve a trip to the veterinarian for treatment. Fortunately, today there are several good products available to help prevent fleas and eliminate them when there is an outbreak.

If there is a flea infestation, no one product is going to correct the problem. Not only will the dog require treatment, but so will the environment. In general, flea collars are not always very effective, although there is an "egg" collar now available that will kill the eggs on the dog. Dips are the most economical, but they are messy. There are some effective shampoos and treatments available through pet shops and veterinarians.

Another popular parasiticide is permethrin, which is applied to the back of the dog in one or two places, depending on the dog's weight. This product works as a repellent, causing the flea to get "hot feet" and jump off. Do not confuse this product with some of the organophosphates that are also applied to the dog's back.

Some products are not usable on young puppies, and treating fleas should be done under your veterinarian's guidance. Frequently, it is necessary to combine products, and the layman does not have enough knowledge regarding possible toxicities. It is hard to believe, but there are a few dogs who do have a natural resistance to fleas. Nevertheless, it would be wise to treat all pets at the same time. Don't forget your cats, either; cats just love to prowl the neighborhood and return with unwanted guests.

The majority of dogs are allergic to the bite of a flea, and in many cases it only takes one fleabite to require treatment.

Adult fleas live on the dog, but their eggs drop off into the environment. There, they go through four larval stages before reaching adulthood, when they are able to jump back on the poor unsuspecting dog. The cycle resumes and takes between 21 to 28 days under ideal conditions. There are environmental products available that will kill both adult fleas and larvae.

Ticks

Ticks can carry Rocky Mountain Spotted Fever, Lyme disease, and can cause tick paralysis. They should be removed with tweezers. Try to pull out the head because the jaws carry disease. Tick preventive collars do an excellent job. Ticks automatically back out on those dogs wearing collars.

Sarcoptic Mange

The mite characterized by sarcoptic mange is difficult to find on skin scrapings. The female mite burrows under the skin and lays her eggs, which hatch within a few days. Sarcoptic mange causes intense itching in dogs and may even be characterized by hair loss in its early stages. Sarcoptes are highly contagious to other dogs and to humans, although they do not live long on humans.

Demodectic Mange

Demodectic mange is a mite that is passed from the dam to her puppies. It commonly affects youngsters aged three to ten months. Diagnosis is confirmed by skin scraping. Small areas of alopecia around the eyes, lips, and/or forelegs become visible. There is little itching unless there is a secondary bacterial infection. Some breeds are afflicted more than others.

Cheyletiella

Cheyletiella causes intense itching and is diagnosed by skin scraping. It lives in the outer layers of the skin of dogs, cats, rabbits, and humans. Yellow-gray scales may be found on the back and the rump, top of the head, and the nose.

OTHER MEDICAL PROBLEMS

Anal Sac Impaction/Inflammation

Anal sacs are small sacs on either side of the rectum that can cause the dog discomfort when they are full. They should empty when the dog has a bowel movement. Symptoms of inflammation or impaction include excessive licking under the tail and/or a bloody or sticky discharge from the anal area. Breeders recommend emptying the sacs on a regular schedule when bathing the dog. Many veterinarians, on the other hand, prefer that this not be done unless there are symptoms.

You can express the sacs by squeezing them (at the five and seven o'clock positions) in and up toward the anus. Take precautions not to get in the way of the foul-smelling fluid that is expressed. Some dogs object to this procedure, so it would be wise to have someone hold your dog's head at this time. Sometimes you will see your dog scooting his rear end along the floor, which is caused by anal sac irritation and not worms.

Colitis

When the stool is blood or blood tinged, it could be the result of inflammation of the colon. Colitis, sometimes intermittent, can be the result of stress, undiagnosed whipworms, or perhaps may be idiopathic (no explainable reason for the condition). If intermittent bloody stools are an ongoing problem, you should probably feed a diet higher in fiber. Seek professional help if your dog seems to be suffering and/or the condition persists.

Conjunctivitis

Many breeds are prone to conjunctivitis. The conjunctiva is the pink tissue that lines the inner surface of the eyeball, with the exception of the clear, transparent cornea. Irritating substances such as bacteria, foreign matter, or chemicals can cause it to become reddened and swollen. It is important to keep any hair trimmed from around the eyes. Long hair stays damp and aggravates the problem. Keep the eyes cleaned with warm water, and wipe away any matter that has accumulated in the corner of the eyes. If the condition persists, you should see your veterinarian. This problem goes hand in hand with keratoconjunctivitis sicca.

Ear Infection

Otitis externa is an inflammation of the external ear canal that begins at the outside opening of the ear and extends inward to the eardrum. Dogs with pendulous ears are prone to this disease, but breeds with upright ears also have a high incidence of problems. Allergies, food, and inhalants, along with hormonal problems, such as hypothyroidism, are major contributors to the disease. For those dogs who have recurring problems, you need to investigate the underlying causes if you hope to cure them.

Be careful never to get water in the ears. Water provides a great medium for bacteria to grow. If your dog swims or you inadvertently get water in his ears, use a drying agent. You can use an at-home preparation of equal parts of 3-percent hydrogen peroxide and 70-percent rubbing alcohol. Another preparation is equal parts of white vinegar and water. As an alternative, your veterinarian can provide a suitable product. When cleaning the ears, use cotton-tip applicators extremely carefully, because they make it easy to pack debris down into the canal. Only clean what you can see.

If your dog has an ongoing infection, don't be surprised if your veterinarian recommends sedating him and flushing his ears with a bulb syringe. Sometimes this needs to be done a few times to get the ear clean. The ear must be clean so that medication can come into contact with the canal. Be prepared to return for checkups until the infection is gone. This may involve more flushing if the ears are badly infected.

For chronic or recurring cases, your veterinarian may recommend thyroid testing, etc., as well as a hypoallergenic diet for a trial period

If your dog is suffering from fleabite allergy, he may need medical attention to ease his discomfort.

of 10 to 12 weeks. Depending on your dog, it may be a good idea to see a dermatologist. Ears shouldn't be taken lightly, because if the condition gets out of hand, surgery may be necessary. Ask your veterinarian to explain proper ear maintenance for your dog.

Fleabite Allergy

Fleabite allergy is the result of a hypersensitivity to the bite of a flea and its saliva. It only takes one bite to cause the dog to chew or scratch himself raw. Your dog may need medical attention to ease his discomfort. You should clip the hair around the "hot spot" and wash it with mild soap and water, and you may need to do this daily if the area weeps. Apply an antibiotic anti-inflammatory product. Hot spots can occur from other trauma as well, such as grooming.

Interdigital Cysts

Check for interdigital cysts on your dog's feet if he shows signs of lameness. They are frequently associated with staph infections and can be quite painful. A home remedy is to soak the infected foot in a solution of 1/2 teaspoon of bleach in a couple of quarts of water. Do this two to three times a day for a couple of days. Check with your veterinarian for an alternative remedy; antibiotics usually work well. If there is a recurring problem, surgery may be required.

Lameness

Lameness may be caused by an interdigital cyst, or it could be caused by a mat between the toes, especially if your dog licks his feet. Sometimes it is hard to determine which leg is affected. If your dog is holding up his leg, you need to see your veterinarian.

Poor Skin

Frequently, poor skin is the result of an allergy to fleas, inhalants, or food. These types of problems usually result in a staph dermatitis. Dogs with food allergies usually show signs of severe itching and scratching, though some dogs with food allergies never itch. Their only symptom is a swelling of the ears with no ear infection. Food allergy may result in recurrent bacterial skin and ear infections. Your veterinarian or dermatologist will recommend a good restricted diet.

Inhalant allergies result in atopy, which causes licking of the feet, scratching of the body, and rubbing of the muzzle. These allergies may be seasonable. Your veterinarian or dermatologist can perform intradermal testing for inhalant allergies. If your dog should test positive, then a vaccine may be prepared.

Tonsillitis

Usually, young dogs have a higher incidence of tonsillitis than older dogs because older dogs have a built-up resistance. It is very contagious. Sometimes it is difficult to determine if the condition is tonsillitis or kennel cough because the symptoms are similar. Symptoms of tonsillitis include fever, poor eating, difficulty swallowing, and retching up a white, frothy mucus.

SPAYING AND NEUTERING

More than likely, your breeder has requested that you have your puppy neutered or spayed. Your breeder's request is based on what is healthiest for your dog and what is most beneficial for your breed. Experienced and conscientious breeders devote many years to developing a bloodline. In order to do this, they make every effort to plan each breeding cycle with regard to conformation, temperament, and health.

A responsible breeder does his or her best to perform the necessary testing (i.e. OFA, CERF, testing for inherited blood disorders, thyroid, etc.). Testing is expensive and sometimes very disheartening when a favorite dog doesn't pass his health tests. The health history pertains not only to the breeding stock but also to the immediate ancestors.

Reputable breeders do not want their offspring to be bred indiscriminately. Therefore, you may be asked to neuter or spay your puppy. Of course, there is always the exception, and the breeder may agree to let you breed your dog under his or her direct supervision. This is an important concept. More and more effort is being made to breed healthier dogs.

The Benefits of Spaying and Neutering

There are numerous benefits to spaying or neutering your dog. Intact males and females may be prone to housetraining accidents. Females urinate frequently before, during, and after heat cycles, and males tend to mark territory if there is a female in heat. Males may show the same behavior if there are guests or a visiting dog. Spaying and neutering may virtually eliminate these behaviors.

Surgery involves a sterile operating procedure equivalent to human surgery. The incision site is shaved, surgically scrubbed, and draped. The veterinarian wears a sterile surgical gown, cap, mask, and gloves. It is customary for the veterinarian to recommend a preanesthetic blood screening, looking for metabolic problems, and an ECG rhythm strip to check for normal heart function. Today, anesthetics are equal to human anesthetics, which means your dog can walk out of the clinic the same day as surgery.

Spaying

Unspayed females are subject to mammary and ovarian cancer. In order to prevent mammary cancer, a female must be spayed prior to her first heat cycle. Later in life, an unspayed female may develop a pyometra (an infected uterus), a life-threatening condition.

Spaying is performed at about six months of age under a general anesthetic and is easy on the young dog. As you might expect, it is a little harder on the older dog, but that is no reason to deny her the surgery. The surgery removes the ovaries and uterus. It is important to remove all of the ovarian tissue. If some is left behind, she could remain attractive to males. In order to view the ovaries, a reasonably long incision is necessary. An ovariohysterectomy is considered major surgery.

Your breeder's request that you spay or neuter your Chihuahua is based on what is healthiest for your dog and best for the breed.

Most dogs who have been spayed or neutered are just as active after the surgery as they were before, keeping weight at a healthy level.

Neutering

Neutering the male at a young age will inhibit some characteristic male behavior that owners frown upon. Some males will not hike their legs and mark territory if they are neutered at six months of age. Also, neutering at a young age has hormonal benefits, lessening the chance of hormonal aggressiveness.

Surgery involves removing the testicles but leaving the scrotum. If there should be a retained testicle, the male definitely needs to be neutered before the age of two or three years, because retained testicles can develop cancer. Unneutered males are at risk for testicular cancer, perineal fistulas, perianal tumors and fistulas, and prostatic disease.

After the Surgery

Some people worry about their dogs gaining weight after being neutered or spayed. This is usually not the case. It is true that some dogs may be less active, so they could develop a problem, but most are just as active as they were before surgery. However, if your dog should begin to gain weight, you need to decrease his or her food and see to it that he or she gets a little more exercise.

SPORT of Purebred Dogs

Welcome to the exciting and sometimes frustrating sport of dogs. Dog showing has been a very popular sport for a long time and has been taken quite seriously by some, while others only enjoy it as a hobby. This section covers the basics that may entice you, further your knowledge, and help you to understand the dog world.

The Kennel Club in England was formed in 1859, the American Kennel Club was established in 1884, and the Canadian Kennel Club was formed in 1888. The purpose of these clubs was to register purebred dogs and maintain their studbooks. In the beginning, the concept of registering dogs was not readily accepted. However,

Dog showing, a sport that requires a great deal of dedication on the parts of both dog and owner, has been popular for a long time.

more than 36 million dogs have been enrolled in the AKC Studbook since its inception in 1888. Presently, the kennel clubs not only register dogs, but they also adopt and enforce rules and regulations governing dog shows, obedience trials, and field trials. Over the years they have fostered and encouraged interest in the health and welfare of the purebred dog. They routinely donate funds to veterinary research for study on genetic disorders.

Today there are numerous activities that are enjoyable for both the dog and the handler. Some of the activities include conformation showing, obedience competition, tracking, agility, the Canine Good Citizen® Program, and a wide range of instinct tests that vary from breed to breed. Where you start depends upon your goals, which early on may not be readily apparent.

PUPPY KINDERGARTEN

Every puppy will benefit from this class. Puppy Kindergarten Training (PKT) is the foundation for all future dog activities, from conformation to "couch potatoes." Pet owners should make an effort to attend, even if they never expect to show their dogs. The class is designed for puppies about three months of age, with graduation at approximately five months of age. All of the puppies will be in the same age group, and even though some may be a little unruly, there should not be any real problem.

The class will teach the puppy some beginning obedience. As in all obedience classes, the owner will learn how to train his or her own dog. The PKT class gives the puppy the opportunity to interact with other puppies in the same age group and exposes him to strangers, which is very important. Without training, some dogs grow up and develop problem behaviors, one of them being fear of strangers. As you can see, there can be much to gain from this class.

CANINE GOOD CITIZEN® PROGRAM

The AKC sponsors a program to encourage dog owners to train their dogs. Local clubs perform the pass/fail tests, and dogs who pass are awarded a Canine Good Citizen® Certificate. Proof of vaccination is required at the time of participation. The test includes:

The American Kennel Club's Canine Good Citizen® program encourages owners to train their dogs.

1. Accepting a friendly stranger.
2. Sitting politely for petting.
3. Appearance and grooming.
4. Walking on a loose leash.
5. Walking through a crowd.
6. Sit and down on command/staying in place.
7. Coming when called.
8. Reaction to another dog.
9. Reactions to distractions.
10. Supervised separation.

CONFORMATION

Conformation showing is the oldest dog show sport. This type of showing is based on the dog's appearance—that is, his structure, movement, and attitude. When considering this type of showing, you need to be aware of your breed's standard and be able to evaluate your dog compared to that standard. The breeder of your puppy or other experienced breeders would be good sources for such an evaluation. Puppies can go through many changes over a period of time. Many puppies start out as promising hopefuls and then after maturing may be disappointing as show candidates. Even so, this should not deter them from being excellent pets.

Local kennel clubs or obedience clubs usually offer conformation training classes. These are excellent places for training puppies. The puppy should be able to walk on a lead before entering such a class. Proper ring procedure and technique for posing (stacking) and gaiting the dog will be demonstrated. Generally, certain patterns are used in the ring, such as the triangle or the "L." Conformation class, like the PKT class, will give your puppy the opportunity to socialize with different breeds of dog as well as humans.

It takes some time to learn the routine of conformation showing. Usually, one starts at the AKC-sanctioned puppy matches or fun matches. These matches are generally for puppies from 2 or 3 months to a year old, and there may be classes for the adult over the age of 12 months. Similar to point shows, the classes are divided by sex, and after completion of the classes in that breed or variety, the class winners compete for Best of Breed or Variety. The winner goes on to compete in the Group, and the Group winners compete for Best in Match. No championship points are awarded for match wins.

A few matches can be great training for puppies, even if you don't intend to go on showing. Matches enable the puppy to meet new people and be handled by a stranger—the judge. They also offer a change of environment, which broadens the horizon for both dog and handler. Matches and other dog activities boost the confidence of the handler, especially the younger handlers.

Conformation in the United States

The AKC championship is built on a point system, which is different from Great Britain. To become an AKC Champion of Record, the dog must earn 15 points. The number of points earned each time depends upon the number of dogs in competition. The number of points available at each show depends upon the breed, its sex, and the location of the show. The US is divided into ten AKC zones. Each zone has its own set of points. The purpose of the zones is to try to equalize the points available from breed to breed and area to area. The AKC adjusts the point scale annually.

The number of points that can be won at a show are between one and five. Three-, four- and five-point wins are considered majors. Not only does the dog need 15 points won under three different judges, but those points must include two majors under two different judges. Canada also works on a point system, but majors are not required.

Males always show before bitches. The classes available to those seeking points are: Puppy (which may be divided into 6 to 9 months and 9 to 12 months); 12 to 18 months; Novice; Bred-by-Exhibitor; American-bred; and Open. The class winners of the same sex of each breed or variety compete against each other for Winners Dog and Winners Bitch. A Reserve Winners Dog and Reserve Winners Bitch are also awarded but do not carry any points unless the original win is disallowed by the AKC. The Winners Dog and Bitch compete with the Specials (those dogs who have attained a championship) for Best of Breed or Variety, Best of Winners, and Best of Opposite Sex. It is possible to pick up an extra point or even a major if the points are higher for the defeated winner than those of Best of Winners. The latter would get the higher total from the defeated winner.

At an all-breed show, each Best of Breed or Variety winner will go on to his respective Group, and then the Group winners will compete against each other for Best in Show. There are seven

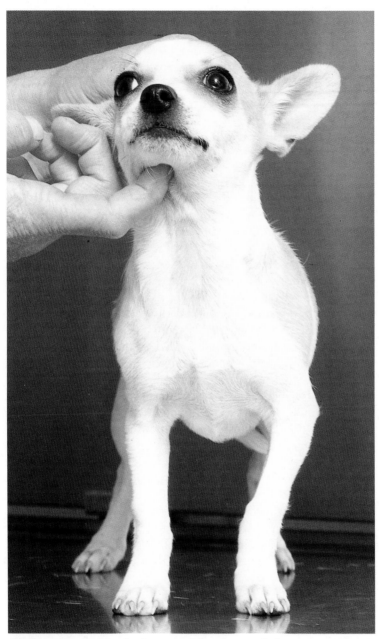

Conformation, the oldest dog show sport, is based upon a dog's structure, movement, and attitude.

Groups: Sporting, Hounds, Working, Terriers, Toys, Non-Sporting, and Herding. Obviously, there are no Groups at specialty shows (those shows that have only one breed or a show such as the American Spaniel Club's Flushing Spaniel Show, which is for all flushing spaniel breeds).

Conformation in England

Earning a championship in England is somewhat different because England does not have a point system. Challenge Certificates are awarded if the judge feels the dog is deserving, regardless of the number of dogs in competition. A dog must earn three Challenge Certificates under three different judges, with at least one of these Certificates being won after the age of 12 months. Competition is very strong, and entries may be higher than they are in the US. The Kennel Club's Challenge Certificates are only available at championship shows.

In England, the Kennel Club regulations require that certain dogs—Border Collies and gundog breeds—qualify in a working capacity (i.e. obedience or field trials) before becoming a Full Champion. If they do not qualify in the working aspect, then they are designated a show champion, which is equivalent to the AKC's Champion of Record. A gundog may be granted the title of Field Trial Champion (FTCh.) if he passes all of the tests in the field, but he would also have to qualify in conformation before becoming a Full Champion. A Border Collie who earns the title of Obedience Champion (ObCh.) must also qualify in the conformation ring before becoming a champion.

The US doesn't have a designation for Full Champion but does award for Dual and Triple Champions. The Dual Champion must be a Champion of Record and either a Champion Tracker, Herding Champion, Obedience Trial Champion, or Field Champion. Any dog who has been awarded the titles of Champion of Record and any two of the following: Champion Tracker, Herding Champion, Obedience Trial Champion, or Field Champion, may be designated as a Triple Champion.

Showing in the United States and England

Conformation shows in England seem to put more emphasis on breeder judges than those in the US. There is much competition within the breeds. Therefore, the quality of the individual breeds

In a conformation show, your Chihuahua will be judged on how closely he adheres to the standard for the breed.

should be very good. In the US, there tend to be more "all-around judges" (those who judge multiple breeds), with breeder judges used at the specialty shows. Breeder judges are more familiar with their own breed, as they are actively breeding that breed or did so at one time. Americans emphasize Group and Best in Show wins and promote them accordingly.

The shows in England can be very large and extend over several days, with the Groups scheduled on different days. Though multi-day shows are not common in the US, there are cluster shows in which several different clubs use the same show site over consecutive days.

Westminster Kennel Club

The Westminster Kennel Club is the most prestigious dog show in the US, although the entry is limited to 2,500. In recent years, entry has been limited to champions. This show is more formal than the majority of the shows, with the judges wearing formal attire and the handlers fashionably dressed. In most instances, the quality of the dogs is superb— after all, it is a show of champions! It is a good show to study the AKC registered breeds and is by far the most exciting—especially because it is televised. Westminster is also one of the few shows in this country that is still benched. This means the dog must be in his benched area during the show hours, except when he is being groomed, is in the ring, or is being exercised.

Typically, the handlers are very particular about their appearances. They are careful not to wear something that will detract from their dogs; instead, they try to wear clothing that will enhance their dogs. American ring procedure is quite formal compared to that of other countries. There is a certain etiquette expected between the judge and exhibitor and among the other exhibitors. Of course, that is not always the case, but the judge is supposed to be polite, not engaging in small talk or acknowledging how well he or she knows the handler. There is a more informal and relaxed atmosphere at the shows in other countries; for instance, the dress code is more casual. The US is very handler-oriented in many of the breeds.

Crufts

In England, Crufts is the Kennel Club's show and is most assuredly the largest dog show in the world. It's been known to have an entry of nearly 20,000, and the show lasts four days. Entry is only gained by qualifying through winning in specified classes at another championship show. Westminster is strictly conformation, but Crufts exhibitors and spectators enjoy not only conformation, but also obedience, agility, and a multitude of exhibitions as well. Obedience was admitted in 1957 and agility in 1983.

Junior Showmanship

The Junior Showmanship Class is a wonderful way to build self-confidence, even if there are no aspirations of staying with dog showing later in life. Frequently, Junior Showmanship becomes the background of those who become successful exhibitors/handlers in the future. In some instances, it is taken very seriously, and success is measured in terms of wins. The Junior Handler is judged solely on his or her ability and skill in presenting his or her dog. The dog's conformation is not to be considered by the judge. Even so, the condition and grooming of the dog may be a reflection upon the handler.

Usually, the matches and point shows include different classes. The Junior Handler's dog may be entered in a breed or obedience class and even shown by another person in that class. Junior Showmanship classes are usually divided by age. The age is determined by the handler's age on the day of the show. The classes are:

- Novice Junior for those at least 10 and under 14 years of age, who at the time of entry closing have not won three first places in a Novice Class at a licensed or member show.

- Novice Senior for those at least 14 and under 18 years of age, who at the time of entry closing have not won three first places in a Novice Class at a licensed or member show.

- Open Junior for those at least 10 and under 14 years of age, who at the time of entry closing have won at least three first places in a Novice Junior Showmanship Class at a licensed or member show with competition present.

- Open Senior for those at least 14 and under 18 years of age, who at the time of entry closing have won at least three first places in a Novice Junior Showmanship Class at a licensed or member show with competition present.

Junior Handlers must include their AKC Junior Handler number on each show entry. This should be obtained from the AKC.

Apparel and Supplies

If you are handling your own dog, please give some consideration to your apparel. The dress code at matches is more informal than at the point shows. However, you should wear something a little more appropriate than beach attire or ragged jeans and bare feet. If you check out the handlers and see what is presently fashionable, you'll catch on. Men usually dress with a shirt and tie and a nice sports coat. Whether you are male or female, you will want to wear comfortable clothes and shoes. You need to be able to run with your dog, and you certainly don't want to take a chance of falling and hurting yourself. Women usually wear a dress or two-piece outfit, preferably with pockets to carry bait, brush, etc. The length of a woman's skirt or dress should be considered in case she needs to kneel on the

Your Chihuahua will need to undergo extensive training if he is to compete in obedience events.

floor, as should the ability of the dress or outfit to provide freedom of movement when running.

If you are showing in obedience, you may want to wear pants. Many top obedience handlers wear pants that are color-coordinated with their dogs. The philosophy is that imperfections in the black dog will be less obvious next to the handler's black pants.

Take the following items to the show with your dog: crate; ex pen (if you use one); extra bedding; water pail and water; all required grooming equipment; table; chair for you; bait for dog and lunch for you and friends; and last but not least, clean-up materials, such as plastic bags, paper towels, and perhaps a damp towel—just in case. Don't forget your entry confirmation and directions to the show.

Whether you are showing in conformation, Junior Showmanship, or obedience, watch the clock and be sure you are not late. It is customary to pick up your conformation armband a few minutes before the start of the class. They will not wait for you, and if you are on the show grounds and not in the ring, you will upset everyone. It's a little more complicated picking up your obedience armband if you show later in the class. If you have not picked it up and they get to your number, you may not be allowed to show. It's best to pick up your armband early, but be aware that you may show earlier than expected if other handlers don't pick up. Customarily, all conflicts should be discussed with the judge prior to the start of the class.

OBEDIENCE

Obedience is necessary, without a doubt, but it can also become a wonderful hobby and even an obsession. Obedience classes and competition can provide wonderful companionship, not only with your dog but also with your classmates or fellow competitors. It is always gratifying to discuss your dog's problems with others who have had similar experiences. The AKC acknowledged obedience around 1936, and it has changed tremendously, even though many of the exercises are basically the same. Today, obedience competition is just that—very competitive. Even so, it is possible for every obedience exhibitor to come home a winner (by earning qualifying scores), even though he or she may not earn a placement in the class.

Most of the obedience titles are awarded after earning three qualifying scores (legs) in the appropriate class under three different judges. These classes offer a perfect score of 200, which is extremely rare. Each of the class exercises has its own point value. A leg is earned after receiving a score of at least 170 and at least 50 percent of the points available in each exercise. The titles are:

Companion Dog—CD

This is called the Novice Class, and the exercises are:

1.	Heel on leash and figure 8	40 points
2.	Stand for examination	30 points
3.	Heel free	40 points
4.	Recall	30 points
5.	Long sit—one minute	30 points
6.	Long down—three minutes	30 points

Maximum total score   200 points

Companion Dog Excellent—CDX

This is the Open Class, and the exercises are:

1.	Heel off leash and figure 8	40 points
2.	Drop on recall	30 points
3.	Retrieve on flat	20 points
4.	Retrieve over high jump	30 points
5.	Broad jump	20 points
6.	Long sit—three minutes (out of sight)	30 points
7.	Long down—five minutes (out of sight)	30 points

Maximum total score   200 points

Utility Dog—UD

The Utility Class exercises are:

1.	Signal exercise	40 points
2.	Scent discrimination-Article 1	30 points
3.	Scent discrimination-Article 2	30 points
4.	Directed retrieve	30 points
5.	Moving stand and examination	30 points
6.	Directed jumping	40 points

Maximum total score   200 points

After achieving the UD title, you may feel inclined to go after the UDX and/or OTCh. The UDX (Utility Dog Excellent) title went into effect in January 1994. It is not easily attained. The title requires qualifying simultaneously ten times in Open B and Utility B, but not necessarily at consecutive shows.

The OTCh. (Obedience Trial Champion) is awarded after the dog has earned his UD and then goes on to earn 100 championship points, a first place in Utility, a first place in Open, and another first place in either class. The placements must be won under three different judges at all-breed obedience trials. The points are determined by the number of dogs competing in the Open B and Utility B classes. The OTCh. title precedes the dog's name.

Obedience matches (AKC-sanctioned, fun, and show-and-go) are often available. Usually, they are sponsored by the local obedience clubs. When preparing an obedience dog for a title, you will find matches very helpful. Fun matches and show-and-go matches are more lenient in allowing you to make corrections in the ring. This type of training is usually very necessary for the Open and Utility classes. AKC-sanctioned obedience matches do not allow corrections in the ring because they must abide by the AKC obedience regulations booklet. If you are interested in showing in obedience, you should contact the AKC for a copy of *Obedience Regulations.*

Agility, a sport that requires both speed and coordination, is a fun event for dogs, handlers, and spectators alike

AGILITY

Agility was first introduced by John Varley at the Crufts Dog Show in England in February 1978, but Peter Meanwell, competitor and judge, actually developed the idea. It was officially recognized in the early 1980s. Agility is extremely popular in England and Canada and is growing in popularity in the US. The AKC acknowledged agility in August 1994. Dogs must be at least 12 months of age to be entered. It is a fascinating sport that the dog, handler, and spectators enjoy to the utmost.

Agility is a spectator sport in which the dog performs off lead. The handler either runs with his or her dog or positions himself or herself on the course. He or she then directs the dog with verbal and hand signals over a timed course, over or through a variety of obstacles, including a time-out or pause. One of the main drawbacks to agility is finding a place to train. The obstacles take up a lot of space, and it is very time consuming to put up and take down courses.

The titles earned at AKC agility trials are Novice Agility Dog (NAD), Open Agility Dog (OAD), Agility Dog Excellent (ADX),

In agility competition, the dog performs off lead and is directed with verbal and hand signals.

Although only recognized by the AKC since 1994, agility is steadily gaining in popularity in the US.

and Master Agility Excellent (MAX). In order to acquire an agility title, a dog must earn a qualifying score in his respective class on three separate occasions under two different judges. The MAX will be awarded after earning ten qualifying scores in the Agility Excellent Class.

GENERAL INFORMATION

Obedience and agility allow the purebred Chihuahua with an Indefinite Listing Privilege (ILP) number or a limited registration to be exhibited and earn titles. Application must be made to the AKC for an ILP number.

The American Kennel Club publishes *Events,* a monthly magazine that is part of the *Gazette,* their official journal for the sport of purebred dogs. The events section lists upcoming shows and the secretary or superintendent for them. The majority of the conformation shows in the US are overseen by licensed superintendents. Generally, the entry closing date is approximately two and a half weeks before the actual show. Point shows are fairly expensive, while the match shows cost about one-third of the point show entry fee. Match shows usually take entries the day of the show, but some are pre-entry. The best way to find match show information is through your local kennel club. Upon request, the AKC can provide you with a list of superintendents, and you can write and ask to be put on their mailing lists.

Obedience trial information is also available through the AKC. Frequently, these events are not superintended, but they are put on by the host club. Therefore, you should make the entry with the event's secretary.

There are numerous activities you can share with your dog. Regardless of what you do, it does take teamwork. Your dog can only benefit from your attention and training.

BEHAVIOR and Canine Communication

S tudies of the human/animal bond point out the importance of the unique relationships that exist between people and their pets. Those of us who share our lives with pets understand the special part they play through companionship, service, and protection. For many, the pet/owner bond goes beyond simple companionship; pets are often considered members of the family.

A leading pet food manufacturer recently conducted a nationwide survey of pet owners to gauge just how important pets were in their lives. Here's what they found:

- 76 percent allow their pets to sleep on their beds
- 78 percent think of their pets as their children
- 84 percent display photos of their pets, mostly in their homes
- 84 percent think that their pets react to their own emotions
- 100 percent talk to their pets
- 97 percent think that their pets understand what they're saying

Pets play a special part in their owners' lives, lending them companionship, service, and protection.

It has been proven that senior citizens show more concern for their own eating habits when given the responsibility of feeding a dog. Further, seeing that their dogs are routinely exercised encourages elderly owners to think of schedules that otherwise may seem unimportant to them. In addition, while the older owner may be arthritic and not feeling well, having a dog may encourage him or her to become more active. Over the last few decades, pets have been shown to relieve the stress of those who lead busy lives, and owning a pet has even been known to lessen the occurrence of heart attack and stroke.

Many single people thrive on the companionship of their dogs. Lifestyles are very different than they used to be, and today more individuals seek the single life. However, they receive fulfillment from dog ownership. The majority of dogs, however, live in family environments. The companionship these pets provide is well worth the effort involved. Children in particular benefit from having a family dog. Dogs teach responsibility through the understanding of their care, feelings, and even respect for their life cycles. Frequently,

Studies show that senior citizens who own dogs take extra care with their own health and well-being.

For many people who own pets, the pet/owner bond goes beyond simple companionship.

those children who have not been exposed to dogs grow up afraid of them. Dogs can sense timidity, and some will take advantage of the situation.

Today, more dogs are working as service dogs, and many dogs are trained to aid the blind and deaf. Also, dogs are trained to provide multiple services for the disabled and are able to perform many different tasks for their owners. Search and rescue dogs, along with their handlers, are sent throughout the world to assist in the recovery of disaster victims. They are lifesavers. Some dogs become therapy dogs and are very popular with nursing homes and hospitals. The inhabitants of these establishments truly look forward to the dogs' visits.

Nationally, there is a Pet Awareness Week to educate students and others about the value and basic care of our pets. Many countries take an even greater interest in their pets than Americans do. In those countries, pets are allowed to accompany their owners into restaurants and shops. In the US, this freedom is only available to service dogs. Even so, people still think very highly of the human/animal bond.

SOCIALIZATION AND TRAINING

Many prospective puppy buyers lack experience regarding the proper socialization and training needed to develop a desirable pet. In the first 18 months, training does take some work, but it is easier to start proper training before there is a problem that needs to be corrected.

The initial work begins with the breeder, who should start socializing the puppy at five to six weeks of age. Human socializing is critical up through 12 weeks of age and is likewise important during the following months. The litter should be left together during the first few weeks, but it is necessary to separate the pups by ten weeks of age. Leaving them together after that time will increase competition for litter dominance. If puppies are not socialized with people by 12 weeks of age, they will be timid later in life.

The eight- to ten-week age period can be a fearful time for puppies. They need to be handled very gently by children and adults. There should be no harsh discipline during this time. Starting at 14 weeks of age, the puppy begins the juvenile period, which ends when he reaches sexual maturity around 6 to 14 months of age. During the juvenile period, he needs to be introduced to

Socialization and training are a crucial part of your dog's development and will enable him to live as part of the family.

strangers (adults, children, and other dogs) on the home property. At sexual maturity, he will begin to bark at strangers and become more protective. A male will start to lift his leg to urinate, but you can inhibit this behavior by walking him on a leash away from trees, shrubs, fences, etc.

Puppy training classes are a great place to socialize your puppy with other dogs and start his training. However, make sure he has all his vaccinations before taking him to meet other dogs. Socialization and training are a crucial part of your dog's development and allow him to live as part of your household and family. In order for your dog to live harmoniously in your home, he should know the household rules. You should always be consistent; this way, your dog will know what is expected of him at all times. Even the most well-trained dogs may exhibit problem behaviors, often due to their natural instincts; for instance, some dogs are very vocal barkers, some dogs are born to dig, and some dogs will run and chase anything that moves. It takes consistent work and patience, but if your dog knows the rules, you can curb problem behaviors and help your dog to become part of the family.

PROBLEM BEHAVIORS

Barking

Barking can be a bad habit learned through the environment, and overzealous barking can be a breed tendency. When barking presents a problem for you, try to stop it as soon as it begins.

To solve barking problems, you first have to determine the cause. Perhaps the barking gets your attention—what your dog considers the perfect reward. If you run and bring him inside when he barks, he then learns that barking gets what he wants—you. He may also be barking because he's protecting your property from perceived (or real) threats, there may be other dogs or children playing nearby, he may be playing, or perhaps he's afraid of something. Again, like digging, some dogs are just more vocal than others and will always be barky, no matter what you do. However, you can control the noise factor through prevention and training.

The best way to stop outside "attention" barking is to ignore him until he realizes barking is futile and he quiets down. If it is bothering the neighbors, bring him inside and crate him, letting him out only when he's quiet.

Yelling at your dog may seem like the thing to do when he's barking, but it's actually counterproductive. To him, your yelling sounds like barking, and when you yell, he will bark more. Yelling just proves to him that the perceived threat is real, or else why would the pack leader be barking too?

If your dog is easily stimulated by what is going on outside, make sure you pull the curtains closed so that he isn't distracted by every leaf that blows by. Do not yell or make a fuss when he does bark. After he barks once or twice, tell him to be quiet and give him praise and a treat when he stops. Soon he will learn that he gets rewards for being quiet, not barking.

If your dog knows your rules, you can curb his problem behaviors.

If your dog is barking inside the house when he is alone, he might be suffering from separation anxiety. A dog who has separation anxiety is inconsolable when you leave the house and will whine, bark, and perhaps scratch at the door. He may also destroy things while you're gone.

In order to help control this problem, don't make a big fuss about saying hello and goodbye when you enter or leave the house. In fact, don't greet your barking dog at all until he has calmed down. Ignore him. When you pet him, you're just rewarding the behavior. Only pet him when he has stopped barking and after you've asked him to sit.

Be sure to crate him or confine him to a safe room when you are gone so that he doesn't get a chance to destroy anything. Turn on the television or radio so that he feels like he has company. Make sure he gets plenty of exercise, and provide him with a chance to eliminate before you leave. Don't forget to give him plenty of chew toys to keep him occupied.

If your dog often barks his head off while in the crate, try this: About 30 minutes before you leave, give him his Nylabone® or a

Rhino® stuffed with peanut butter or cheese, and then ignore him just as if you were already gone. Don't talk to him, and don't say good-bye; just leave. (This also works if you don't leave your dog in a crate.) When you return, don't say hello or make a big deal about coming home; just walk right past the crate and ignore him for about five minutes. When he quiets down, take him directly outside to relieve himself. Don't take him out of the crate when he's barking. The rationale behind this is that if you acknowledge your dog the minute you get home, he'll anticipate your return and bark the entire time you're gone.

Another solution for barking due to separation anxiety is to pretend you're leaving as an exercise to get your dog used to your comings and goings. Place your dog in the crate, put on your coat, take your car keys, and walk around the house for a few minutes. Then, let him out if he's quiet and praise him. Next, dress up again and walk out the door for 30 seconds. Do it again for 2 minutes, then for 5 minutes, then for 10 minutes, then for 20 minutes, and so on. If he's quiet when you return, praise him verbally. If he's barking, just ignore him until he calms down, even if it's only for a moment. Repeat this exercise over a period of several days to several weeks, and your dog should get used to you leaving him.

Jumping Up

A dog who jumps up is a happy dog. Nevertheless, few guests appreciate dogs jumping on them.

Some trainers believe in allowing the puppy to jump up when he is a few weeks old. If you correct him too soon and at the wrong age, you may intimidate him, and he could be timid around humans later in life. However, there will come a time, probably around four months of age, when he needs to know when it is okay to jump and when he is to show good manners by sitting instead.

If you become irritated when your dog jumps up on you, then you should discourage it from the beginning. Jumping can actually cause harm or injury, especially to senior citizens or children. How, though, do you correct the problem? First, all family members need to participate in teaching the puppy to sit as soon as he starts to jump up. The sit must be practiced every time he does it. Don't forget to praise him for his good behavior. Let him know that he only gets petted if he sits first. If he gets up while being petted, stop petting him and tell him to sit again. Tell everyone in the household

To prevent your Chihuahua from running away, he should never be off leash except when supervised in a fenced-in yard.

and anyone who visits not to touch your dog or give him any attention unless he earns it by sitting first.

If your dog is a really bad jumper, ask friends to help as well. Keep dog treats by the door, and ask your visitors to tell your dog to sit when they come over. Keep him on his leash to help him remain under control, and have your guests give him the treat when he sits nicely. With time and patience, he will soon be sitting to greet everyone. Remember, the entire family must take part. Each time you allow your dog to jump up, you go back a step in training.

Running Away

There is little excuse for a dog to run away, because dogs should never be off leash except when supervised in a fenced-in yard.

Many prospective owners want to purchase a female because they believe a male is inclined to roam. It is true that an intact male is inclined to roam, which is one of the reasons a male should be neutered. However, females will roam also, especially if they are in heat. Regardless, these dogs should never be given this opportunity.

The first thing to remember is not to discipline your dog when you finally catch him after an escape. The reasoning behind this is that it is quite possible there could be a repeat performance, and you don't want your dog to be afraid to come to you when you call him.

Always kneel down when trying to catch a runaway. Dogs are afraid of people standing over them. Also, it would be helpful to have a treat or a favorite toy to help entice him to your side. After that initial runaway experience, start practicing the recall with your dog.

Chewing

From 3 to 12 months of age, puppies chew on everything. In fact, they will chew shoes, newspapers, a neighbor's fingers—anything they can get their teeth on. Puppies don't chew out of spite or boredom; it's simply a natural behavior, relieving tension and anxiety. It's also just plain fun! In addition, puppies have to chew because their teeth and gums hurt while they are teething.

Stop your dog from chewing the wrong things by only allowing him to chew on his own toys. Never give him your old shoes, slippers, or socks—he won't be able to distinguish a new pair from an old one. Nylabone® products are great chew toys for both puppies and older dogs. Confining your dog to a crate whenever

Chewing is a natural behavior for dogs, one that relieves tension and anxiety and alleviates the pain associated with teething.

you can't keep an eye on him and puppy proofing your home will also help stop your dog from chewing on things he shouldn't. Remember, puppies *have* to chew. Even after their adult teeth come in, dogs chew to clean and massage their teeth and gums. Give them a safe alternative.

Biting, Nipping, and Mouthing

Biting, mouthing, and nipping are unacceptable behaviors, even in young dogs. What may seem cute in a little pup is not going to be so cute when he gets bigger.

Remember that rough play, wrestling, and tug-of-war aggravate and even teach these unwanted behaviors. Teasing your pup and playing chasing games can also encourage nipping. Your pup has an innate response to hunt and hold onto things. A simple game of tug-of-war means a lot more to your pup than it does to you.

When your puppy nips or bites you, snatch your hand away and say, "No! Ouch!" Then, stop playing with him and ignore him. If your puppy is really overexcited and won't calm down, put him in his crate. Your puppy must realize that you will only play with him and have fun with him if he plays nicely.

Also, be very careful when your puppy is playing with children. Kids can get just as overexcited as puppies do, and the games can get out of hand. Always supervise children and dogs when they are together, and if it gets too rough, institute a "time-out" and confine both the puppy and the child before someone gets hurt. Only let them play if they can be calm around each other.

Aggression

Any act of aggression on your puppy's part should be considered serious. Remember, your cute growling puppy may be an intimidating growling dog one day. If you socialize your puppy properly, you should not have an aggression problem. Remember, do not participate in or allow rough play or wrestling, and don't praise your puppy for nipping.

Your puppy may become possessive regarding various things: his territory, his owners, or his food, or he might show aggression when he is scared. This is where training comes in handy. Your puppy

Proper socialization when your Chihuahua is a puppy will reduce the likelihood that he will become fearful or aggressive as an adult.

must realize from the beginning that where he lives is *your* house and he is living by *your* rules. A pup who thinks he has to protect everything, including you, will be aggressive, and for good reason— he's got a big job. But if you teach him from the beginning that you are the leader, you shouldn't have a problem.

Your dog should let you take things away from him or approach his food bowl. He should not growl or snap. That bowl is *your* bowl, and that food is *your* food—you should be able to approach anytime you'd like. If you have this problem, approach the bowl with a treat; this will condition your dog to view you approaching the bowl as something pleasant. Keep doing it often, and always praise him when he gives things up. Then, make sure you give those things back to him as his reward for sharing.

Counter Surfing and Trash Spreading

Dogs jump up on tables because they are often rewarded with a tasty dinner, and the scents in your trash cans are just too hard to resist for most dogs. This behavior is best dealt with by preventing it in the first place. Don't give your dog human food, or if you're a softie, put the morsel in his dish and don't let him see that it has come from the counter or the table.

Good management will help to control this behavior. Avoid the counter problem by confining the dog and keeping him out of the kitchen or dining area when you can't supervise him. The simplest way to avoid a "trash hound" is to move the trash out of your dog's reach or buy a trash can with a cover that locks.

If your dog does get into the food he shouldn't, only correct him if you catch him in the act. Just like with housetraining, your dog won't associate the punishment with the food he stole an hour ago or the trash he knocked over this morning. Just chalk it up to experience and practice good management in the future.

Digging

Dogs dig because they're programmed to dig. Terriers, for example, "go to ground," meaning that they find prey in holes in the earth. To them, digging is fun and natural. Some dogs dig because they want to get out of a confined area, and others dig to release pent-up energy. They also dig to get away from the heat, so make sure your dog has plenty of drinking water and shady shelter when he's outside.

If you have a particularly stubborn digger, you can fence off the places where you don't want him to dig and allocate a place in your yard where the dog will be allowed to dig. Let him know that it's okay for him to dig there by bringing him over to the spot and placing a toy or treat on the ground. Later, put it slightly under the dirt and maybe help him dig. When you catch him digging in the wrong place, bring him to his digging place. Show your approval by praising his digging in the right spot.

Stool Eating

Puppies do eat their own stool and even the stool of other animals. This is called coprophagia. It's not the most pleasant of things, but it's a normal habit, and most pups get over it as they grow older. The best solution is to keep your yard really clean and take away the opportunity for your dog to eat anything he shouldn't. However, talk to your veterinarian, and after you have determined that it's not a medical condition or a health problem, ask him or her to prescribe a medicine that makes the waste taste terrible. You can also spray his waste with a bitter apple spray or vinegar—or both. If your pup gets into your cat's litter box, consider moving the box to another location. Sometimes changing a dog's diet and feeding him twice a day will stop coprophagia.

Submissive Urination

Some puppies urinate when they're particularly excited, like when you come home. Most pups who do this will grow out of the behavior in time. However, submissive dogs aren't urinating when the owner comes home because they are excited—they urinate because the leader has engaged them with some form of dominance, such as establishing eye contact, petting on the head and neck, or bending over them. The submissive wolf in the wild would immediately roll over and wet himself when challenged even slightly by a dominant member of the pack. Because you are the dominant member of your pack, the submissive wetter is just doing what seems natural.

The best way to treat this problem is by confining the dog to an area where he can't greet you or your guests right away—he has to get used to new stimuli gradually. Like with separation anxiety, make your comings and goings as low key as possible so the dog doesn't get overly excited.

If your Chihuahua enjoying digging up your garden, fence that area off and offer him an alternative digging location.

Use treats instead of praise for successful greetings (no wetting). Manage the greeting of guests in a controlled area where wetting is okay (outside), and have the dog on a leash and in a sit so that he can't charge the guests in his excitement. Praise, praise, praise for each success, and have patience. The gentler you are to a dog who has this problem, the faster he will overcome it.

Carsickness

Carsickness usually starts during puppyhood, but if you train your puppy to enjoy riding in a car, you may avoid it. There are several causes of carsickness; the most common are the motion of the car, excitement, and anxiety.

Introduce your dog to the car gradually, while he's still young. Don't feed him just before or just after the ride. To accustom him to the car, put him in it and praise him calmly, then take him out and praise him again, without going anywhere. Give him a treat if he'll take it. Follow this routine a few times until he begins to relax.

Now, put him back in the car and start the engine. After a minute, turn it off, take the puppy out, and play with him. Do this a few times, then take him for a short ride, perhaps halfway down the street. Again, play with him afterward. Do this training over an extended period of time when you're not in a rush.

When your dog becomes calm in the car, take him to the park or someplace that's fun for him. Remember that if he only rides in the car on the way to the veterinarian or to be dropped off at the boarding kennel, he might view the car as a negative experience.

Remember to make riding in the car an enjoyable experience. If possible, put him in a crate; he'll be more comfortable there than sitting between a couple of rowdy kids. There are even seat belts made for dogs. Make sure the car is not too hot, and never, ever leave your dog in the car with the windows closed, not even for two minutes. Besides being against the law, your dog could die of heatstroke.

Excessive Fear

Some dogs experience excessive fear directed toward a variety of events, like loud noises and other strange phenomena. The dog may beg to be held, or he may tremble in the corner or hide under the bed, looking around for any kind of comfort. While you may be tempted to coddle and soothe him, try to refrain from doing so. The

Understanding your dog's behavior will help both of you form a loving, lasting relationship.

problem with soothing a terrified dog is that it rewards his behavior—the exaggerated fear. He may learn that there is indeed something to be afraid of, and he'll remember that.

When dealing with excessive fear, it is best to ignore the dog when he's afraid for no good reason. If you must acknowledge his terror, just give him a little pat on the head, tell him it's going to be okay, and then go about your business. Give him a treat, or put the treats on the object he's afraid of if possible so that he associates it with positive things.

TRAVELING With Your Chihuahua

The earlier you start traveling with your new puppy or dog, the better. He needs to become accustomed to traveling. When taking a trip, give consideration to what is best for your dog—traveling with you or boarding. When traveling by car, van, or motor home, you need to think ahead about locking your vehicle. In all probability, you have many valuables in the car and do not wish to leave it unlocked. Perhaps most valuable and not replaceable is your dog. Give a good deal of thought to securing your vehicle and providing adequate ventilation for your pet.

Other considerations when taking a trip with your dog are medical problems that may arise. Little inconveniences may also occur, such as exposure to external parasites. Some areas of the

Because some areas of the country are flea infested, it's a good idea to travel with flea spray.

If your Chihuahua cannot accompany you on a trip, he may be more comfortable at home with a pet-sitter.

country are quite flea infested, so you may want to carry flea spray with you. This is even a good idea when staying in motels; quite possibly you are not the only occupants of the room.

Many motels and even hotels do allow canine guests, even some first-class establishments. There are many good books available that will tell you which hotels accept dogs and also help you plan a fun vacation with your canine companion. Call ahead to any motel or hotel that you may be considering and see if they accept pets. Sometimes it is necessary to pay a deposit against room damage. The management may feel reassured if you mention that your dog will be crated. If you do travel with your dog, take along plenty of plastic bags so that you can clean up after him. As a matter of fact, you should practice cleaning up everywhere you take your dog.

Depending on where you're traveling, you may need an up-to-date health certificate issued by your veterinarian. It is good policy to take along your dog's medical information, which would include the name, address, and phone number of your veterinarian, a vaccination record, rabies certificate, and any medication he is taking.

CAR RIDES

Some dogs are nervous riders and become carsick easily, so it is helpful if your dog starts any trip with an empty stomach. If you continue taking him with you on short, fun rides, it will help accustom him to this experience more smoothly. Older dogs who tend to get carsick may have more of a problem adjusting to traveling. Those dogs who are having serious problems may benefit from medication prescribed by the veterinarian. Also, make sure to give your dog a chance to relieve himself before getting into the car. It is a good idea to be prepared for a cleanup with a leash, paper towels, bag, and terry cloth towel.

When in the car, the safest place for your dog is in a fiberglass or wire crate, such as the Nylabone® Fold-Away Pet Carrier, although close confinement can promote carsickness in some dogs. An alternative to the crate is a car harness made for dogs and/or a safety strap attached to the harness or collar. Whatever you do, do not let your dog ride in the back of a pickup truck unless he is securely tied on a very short lead. If the vehicle stops abruptly, the dog could fall out and be dragged if the lead is too long.

When traveling in the car, the safest place for your dog is in a crate, such as the Nylabone® Fold-Away Pet Carrier.

Another advantage of the crate is that it is a safe place to leave your dog if you need to run into the store. Otherwise, you wouldn't be able to leave the windows down. However, in some states, it is against the law to leave a dog in the car unattended.

Never leave a dog loose in the car wearing a collar and leash. More than one dog has killed himself by hanging. Also, do not let him put his head out an open window. Foreign debris can be blown into his eyes. When leaving your dog unattended in a car, consider the temperature. It can take less than five minutes to reach temperatures over 100°F.

When your Chihuahua is not traveling with you, make sure that he is being cared for by a reputable boarding kennel or pet-sitter.

Air Travel

When traveling by air, you need to contact the airlines to check their policy regarding flying with your dog on board. Usually, you have to make arrangements up to a couple of weeks in advance when traveling with your dog. The airlines require your dog to travel in an airline-approved fiberglass crate. These can be purchased through the airlines, but they are also readily available in most pet-supply stores. The Nylabone® Fold-Away Pet Carrier is a perfect crate for air travel.

If your dog is not accustomed to a crate, it is a good idea to get him acclimated to it before your trip. The day of the actual trip you should withhold serving him water for about 1 hour ahead of departure and refrain from giving him food for about 12 hours. The airlines generally have temperature restrictions that do not allow pets to travel if it is either too cold or too hot. Frequently, these restrictions are based on the temperatures at the departure and arrival airports.

It's best to inquire about a health certificate. These usually need to be issued within ten days of departure. You should arrange for nonstop, direct flights, and if a commuter plane is involved, check to see if it will carry dogs. Some don't. The Humane Society of the United States has put together a tip sheet for airline traveling. You can receive a copy by sending a self-addressed, stamped envelope to:

The Humane Society of the United States
Tip Sheet
2100 L Street NW
Washington, DC 20037

Regulations differ for traveling outside of the country and are sometimes changed without notice. You need to write or call the appropriate consulate or agricultural department for instructions well in advance of your trip. Some countries have lengthy quarantines (six months), and many differ in their rabies vaccination requirements. For instance, it may have to be given at least 30 days ahead of your departure.

Do make sure your dog is wearing proper identification, including your name, phone number, and city. You never know when you might be in an accident and separated from your dog, or your dog could be frightened and somehow manage to escape and run away.

Another suggestion would be to carry in-case-of-emergency instructions. These would include the address and phone number of a relative or friend, your veterinarian's name, address, and phone number, and your dog's medical information.

BOARDING KENNELS

Perhaps you have decided that you need to board your dog. Your veterinarian can recommend a good boarding facility or possibly a pet-sitter who will come to your house. It is customary for the boarding kennel to ask for proof of vaccination for the DHLPP, rabies, and bordetella vaccines. The bordetella should have been given within six months of boarding. This is for your protection. If the boarding kennel does not ask for this proof, you probably should not board at that kennel. Also, ask about flea control. Those dogs who suffer from fleabite allergy can get in trouble at a boarding kennel. Unfortunately, boarding kennels are limited as to how much they are able to do.

Some pet clinics have technicians who pet-sit and board clinic patients in their homes. This may be an alternative for you. Ask your veterinarian if he or she has an employee who can help you. There is a definite advantage to having a technician care for your dog, especially if he is a senior citizen or on medication.

IDENTIFICATION and Finding the Lost Dog

COLLARS AND TAGS

There are several ways of identifying your dog. The old standby is a collar with dog license, rabies tag, and ID tags. Unfortunately, collars have a way of being separated from dogs, and tags fall off, so it's important that they remain intact and on the dog. Collars and tags are the quickest form of identification.

TATTOOS

For several years, owners have been tattooing their dogs. Some tattoos use a number with a registry. Herein lies the problem, because there are several registries to check. If you wish to tattoo your dog, use your social security number. Humane shelters have the means to trace it.

Tattooing is usually done on the inside of the rear thigh. The area is first shaved and numbed. There is no pain, although some dogs do not like the buzzing sound. Occasionally, tattooing is not legible and needs to be redone.

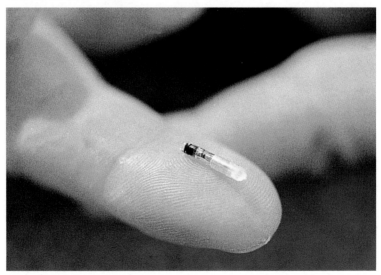

Microchipping, the newest method of identification, is the safest way of identifying your dog.

Your Chihuahua's safety is an enormous responsibility that cannot be taken lightly.

MICROCHIPS

The newest method of identification is microchipping. The microchip is a computer chip that is no larger than a grain of rice. The veterinarian implants it by injection between the shoulder blades. The dog feels no discomfort. If your dog is lost and picked up by the humane society, they can trace you by scanning the microchip, which has its own code. Most microchip scanners are friendly to other brands of microchips and their registries. The microchip comes with a dog tag saying that the dog is microchipped. It is the safest way of identifying your dog.

FINDING THE LOST DOG

Most people would agree that losing a dog is a tragedy. Responsible pet owners rarely lose their dogs because they keep them on a leash or in an enclosed yard. However, even dogs who are in fenced-in yards can get loose. Dogs find ways to escape either over or under fences. Another fast exit may be through the gate that perhaps someone left unlocked.

Below is a list that will hopefully be of help to you if you lose your pet. Remember, don't give up—keep looking. Your dog is worth your efforts.

1. Contact your neighbors and put flyers with a photo on them in their mailboxes. Include information like the dog's name, breed, sex, color, age, source of identification, when your dog was last seen and where, and your name and phone numbers. It may be helpful to say that the dog needs medical care. Offer a reward.

2. Check all local shelters daily. It is also possible that your dog may be picked up away from home and might end up in an out-of-the-way shelter. Check these, too. Go in person; it is not enough to call. Most shelters are limited on the time they can hold dogs before they are put up for adoption or euthanized. There is also the possibility that your dog will not make it to the shelter for several days. He could have been wandering or someone may have tried to keep him.

3. Notify all local veterinarians. Call and send flyers.

4. Call your breeder. Frequently, breeders are contacted when one of their dogs is found.

A securely fenced-in yard will prevent your Chihuahua from running away and becoming lost.

5. Contact the rescue group for your breed.

6. Contact local schools—children may have seen your dog.

7. Post flyers at schools, grocery stores, gas stations, convenience stores, veterinary clinics, groomers, and any other places that will allow them.

8. Advertise in the newspaper.

9. Advertise on the radio.

RESOURCES

BREED CLUBS

British Chihuahua Club
Secretary: Mrs. C. Towler
E-mail: coriam@tiscali.co.uk
www.the-british-chihuahua-
club.org.uk

The Chihuahua Club of America
Secretary: Tanya Delaney
E-mail: Elfin987@aol.com
www.chihuahuaclubofamerica.com

ORGANIZATIONS

American Kennel Club (AKC)
5580 Centerview Drive
Raleigh, NC 27606
Telephone: (919) 233-9767
Fax: (919) 233-3627
E-mail: info@akc.org
www.akc.org

*Association of Pet Dog Trainers
(APDT)*
5096 Sand Road SE
Iowa City, IA 52240-8217
Telephone: (800) PET-DOGS
Fax: (856) 439-0525
E-mail: information@apdt.com
www.apdt.com

Canadian Kennel Club (CKC)
89 Skyway Avenue, Suite 100
Etobicoke, Ontario
M9W 6R4
Telephone: (416) 675-5511
Fax: (416) 675-6506
E-mail: information@ckc.ca
www.ckc.ca

Delta Society
875 124th Ave NE, Ste 101
Bellevue, WA 98005
Telephone: (425) 226-7357
Fax: (425) 235-1076
E-mail: info@deltasociety.org
www.deltasociety.org

The Kennel Club
1 Clarges Street
London
W1J 8AB
Telephone: 0870 606 6750
Fax: 0207 518 1058
www.the-kennel-club.org.uk

United Kennel Club (UKC)
100 E. Kilgore Road
Kalamazoo, MI 49002-5584
Telephone: (269) 343-9020
Fax: (269) 343-7037
E-mail: pbickell@ukcdogs.com
www.ukcdogs.com

RESOURCES

PUBLICATIONS

AKC Family Dog
American Kennel Club
260 Madison Avenue
New York, NY 10016
Telephone: (800) 490-5675
E-mail: familydog@akc.org
www.akc.org/pubs/familydog

Dogs Monthly
Ascot House
High Street, Ascot,
Berkshire SL5 7JG
United Kingdom
Telephone: 1344 628 269
Fax: 1344 622 771
E-mail: admin@rtc-
associates.freeserve.co.uk
www.corsini.co.uk/dogsmonthly

ANIMAL WELFARE GROUPS AND RESCUE ORGANIZATIONS

*American Society for the
Prevention of Cruelty to Animals
(ASPCA)*
424 E. 92nd Street
New York, NY 10128-6804
Telephone: (212) 876-7700
www.aspca.org

*Royal Society for the Prevention of
Cruelty to Animals (RSPCA)*
Telephone: 0870 3335 999
Fax: 0870 7530 284
www.rspca.org.uk

*The Humane Society of the United
States (HSUS)*
2100 L Street, NW
Washington DC 20037
Telephone: (202) 452-1100
www.hsus.org

VETERINARY RESOURCES

*American Veterinary Medical
Association (AVMA)*
1931 North Meacham Road-
Suite 100
Schaumburg, IL 60173
Telephone: (847) 925-8070
Fax: (847) 925-1329
E-mail: avmainfo@avma.org
www.avma.org

*British Veterinary Association
(BVA)*
7 Mansfield Street
London
W1G 9NQ
Telephone: 020 76366541
Fax: 020 74362970
E-mail: bvahq@bva.co.uk
www.bva.co.uk

INDEX